Earrings On Safari

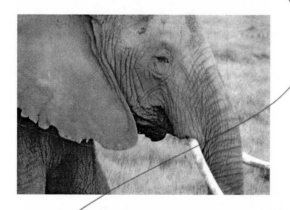

"Marry me and I'll take you around the world."

I did and he did.

We went to Ethiopia.

E-thi-o-pi-a.

Dannie Russell

the Peppertree Press
Sarasota, Florida

Dedication

This book is dedicated to my husband, my forever partner,
who initiated the trips and the jobs in Africa.
To my kids who endure my obsession with all things Africa.
To my writing colleagues who read chapters in Sarasota,
Kampala and three groups in Dubai in 2005 and 2014.

To all who love Africa: its wildlife,
its landscape and its people.

Contents

Prologue

They say, those who play together stay together. They say, if you can travel through Africa as a family, as a couple, you can travel anywhere. After fifty-five years together, Daryle and I are still bumming around Africa and loving it. Together.

"Marry me and I'll take you around the world." I did and he did. I was thinking London, Paris, Rome. We went to Ethiopia. E-thi-o-pi-a. I had to look it up. It was our introduction to Africa and we never looked back.

It was scary for my mum. My dad told me, "You are throwing your life away." He paid for my university studies and saw my education dissolving, like Little Sambo's tigers, in a melted pool at the base of the tree.

When I completed *Home Is Where My Earrings Are* I realized I had written nothing about Africa. Nothing about the continent we love on so many levels.

This volume represents a lifetime of travel in Africa. Privileged to live and work there twice, we've taken the liberty and luxury of traversing the continent over the past five decades. I've always disliked the term *tourist*, preferring to see myself as a traveler. In the words of Pico Iyer, "We *travel*, initially, to lose ourselves; and we *travel*, next, to find ourselves."

While I enjoy finding myself in the slow lane, my energized partner charges forward on the fast track, wanting to never miss a thing, never miss a beat.

"Marry me and I'll take you around the world."

I did and he did.

Africa was our…what: our platform, our launch pad, our go-to refuge, our sometimes jobs, often our haven and retreat. We are still bumming around Africa.

Earrings On Safari

There is no Foo Bird in Africa. There are long legged ostrich and secretary birds and short legged guinea fowl and francolin. There are peacocks, crowned cranes, rollers and bustards; hornbill, plover, starlings and squatty, black vultures that saunter like crones dressed in Goth. The Foo Bird is invented.

The following compilation of stories, told from the perspective of the narrator and sometimes illuminated from the point of view of Mizz Dannie and her Mister, offers anecdotal accounts based on experiences and reflections of the extraordinary continent of Africa.

I believe now, in retrospect, the thread to these pieces is the mighty elephant:

the creature of enormous ears,
elongated proboscis
and weighty body
supported by four
steady
sturdy
pillars.

Because of its strength and memory, its wisdom and psychological sensitivity, the massive elephant represents much of the continent. It symbolizes by *contrast* the smallness, the frailty, the poverty of Africa. The opening story *Safari*, verges on fiction although based on an actual event at Fothergill Island in Zimbabwe. While the episode is true, I took liberties to embellish the characters.

This compilation is a work of nonfiction. If challenged, Mizz Dannie will claim it is all fiction, made the whole thing up, confident her Mister will back her. One exception: the story of Osh is untrue. There is no Osh, but I spent much time on research of

Stone Age tools. While we found many hand carved implements on the flatbeds of Saudi Arabia, in Africa we found carved flint arrowheads, of glistening *black* flint, at Devil's Gate in Kenya.

Stories of camping as well as living on the African continent are meant to show the diversity and also the uniformity of the area from Angola to Zimbabwe. This perspective is presented candidly as a *mzungu*. Yet no *mzungu* can know the continent as a local, and there is no attempt here to know the landmass, its wildlife, its culture with that fervor of intimacy. Going native was never my intent.

We drifted in feluccas along the Nile, climbed the pyramids outside Cairo, descended the underground churches of Lalibela, hewn-from-solid-rock; we poked the ground for giant mushrooms in the forests of South Africa. The continent, like the elephant, is huge, wrinkled, diverse, and is both accessible and inaccessible.

It was on a mini hike at the base of Mount Kenya near the Naro Moro River that Mizz Dannie told the ancient oldest story of the Foo Bird. She said, "I know about Africa," and continued.

"A missionary traveled to a small remote village somewhere on the vast continent of Africa. As he and his family arrived, they were greeted by the whole animated village, the chief being the most jubilant. Young girls and women danced in celebration singing and chanting a song. The missionary noticed that the chorus repeated the syllable "foo" over and over.

The village chief told the missionary that he was just in time for the "Foo Festival," a time of respect and tribute for a local bird, revered as powerful and godlike. The missionary smiled and nodded at the myths of the simple village people. He asked to learn more about the Foo Bird.

The chief said, "Bird small. Known for plentiful feces."

The missionary was taken aback. He waited for embellishment.

"Whole village covered with dried Foo doo," he said to the missionary. "It is great honour for Foo Bird to fly over your hut and bless your roof with droppings." He bowed slightly in respect, leaning on a walking stick as he talked. "Foo poo brings good fortune and blessings." Then, adding the obvious, "It would be a sin to disturb the piles of Foo poo that have accumulated everywhere."

The missionary attempted to process the new culture and customs. He began to say something to the chief when he heard a tiny "chirp." A blob of bird doody landed on his shoulder. He looked up to see the Foo Bird ready to drop another load.

Disgusted, the missionary looked around. He took out his handkerchief and wiped away the Foo feces.

He dropped dead on the spot.

The chief looked at the stricken family and said sadly, "Truly it is written: if the Foo sh*ts, wear it."

———— ✳ ✳ ✳ ————

These pieces do not represent political analysis of the countries of Africa. Not even Mizz Dannie shouted out her critique. It is hoped the stories show reflection and perhaps a personal growth over a fifty year span from our first visit, a two year assignment in Addis Ababa in 1963, to our contracted year in Kampala 2010 nearly fifty years later.

The final chapters summarize thoughts of Uganda from the sprawling, mud entrenched bird market at Nakasero to the successful rhino sanctuary with twenty-four hour rifle protection in the resident rhino reserve, including protection of the beloved Obama and Nandi. It contains a story regarding the takeover of Idi Amin. The characters have been embellished but the story is based on actual accounts. As we left Uganda I gathered up guinea fowl feathers to be divided between fishing lures for the Mister and ever-so-coveted earrings for Mizz Dannie.

There are no Foo feathers. There is no Foo Bird in Africa.

Safari

They were never a close family. He seldom felt connected to either of his parents. When Andrew wanted to express something he went to his sketch pad not knowing what might evolve. He owned volumes of drawing books filled with pencil sketches, pen and inks and oil pastels. Occasionally, he took a finished piece from one of the notebooks to save in the bottom drawer of the dresser. Some pieces he tacked on his bedroom wall. Only a few did he ever frame with proper mounting. When he felt particularly expressive, he might share an illustration with his mother, who politely acknowledged his work.

She never understood his need for art. Andrew knew his mother often worried about him, though he didn't understand why. His father was even less sympathetic toward his constant sketching and his portfolio, embarrassed to tell office mates his son, now sixteen, sat around drawing pictures, messing about with bits of colour.

As a barrister, Ian Stanley, Andrew's father, was well known in London legal circles. He spoke with eloquent speech, both persuasive and loquacious and was active in the community. In constant demand, he addressed service organizations on his interest in wildlife and endangered species. They enjoyed a large home; they lived in comfort. The son did not fit the father's image of a barrister's child. He viewed Andrew as an embarrassment to himself and to his perceived status in the community.

He knew it was a difficult age for his son. The boy seemed to have no self-esteem. There was the issue of his hair. Even the lad's mother made occasional remarks about his hair. The Americans endured their 'grunge,' the British suffered their 'punk.' Indeed, punk would have been a more interesting look. It might signify that he cared about *some* thing; that he struggled to be or identify with something or someone, or whatever those street kids struggled for. His son catered to no particular look. His hair, straight and clean, hung from a cowlick in the center of his head; the untwisted dreads dusted his shoulders. He spoke in tenor. His dark hair accentuated his fair skin. He was pretty.

The adolescent was not interested in football or cricket but he enjoyed being outdoors. After class and on weekends he often took long walks to find an interesting, quiet place to sit and sketch. He liked to observe in the city as well, trying to capture the motion and energy of a street scene. He was good at his sketches. The instructors told him so. But they also made it clear to him that it was his A-Levels he needed to work on, and his father was adamant on this point. "Put down that bloody charcoal and hit the books, lad," he admonished on those rare occasions they were together. Well at least the kid wasn't glued to a screen as he had read about American youth culture.

The inspiration came to the father during a speech to the Rotary Club: this year they would travel together, just father and son, a journey to Africa, a safari. Africa. Every man's dream: the thrill and excitement of being in the wild, the study of the environment and ecosystems; manhood discovered. He wanted a way to be close to his son, but never found a link, a way to connect. He closed-up when office mates talked about their daughters and sons; left the room for a cupa. His fear was that Andrew was serious about art. Drawing was not a vocation, not a legitimate career.

* * *

Andrew and his father stepped out of the open Land Rover shuttle and followed the tall thin porter who carried their khaki-brown, newly purchased safari-duffels. They walked past the gift shop, past the lodge where guests milled about, already sporting "Save The Rhino" T-shirts.

The lodge projected a relaxed ambiance. Guests lingered over afternoon tea nibbling slices of lemon sponge cake in anticipation of late-in-the-day safaris; the lodge, a collage of young couples, loud-voiced, loud-shirted American groups, Australian retirees, the inevitable Japanese with sun hats and thick-strapped cameras, occasional pads held up as lenses, plus African families on holiday. On printed souvenir lists, visitors checked-off animals already seen and circled those they hoped to observe during their holiday.

Guests wrote notes on spectacular picture postcards which suggested it was their own photo, scenes they anticipated and were certain their sure-shot, mostly new, digital cameras would capture. Some wrote copious notes in their once-in-a-lifetime diaries. And to be sure that it was all recorded, emails flew in orbit and everyone texted someone. It might be the bush, but it was enabled; access available bush.

Down a narrow dirt path, their thatched-roof *banda* blended into the environment, nestled-in amongst tall eucalyptus trees. Monkeys hovered high-up in the branches. This was safari.

The lanky African placed the bags inside the bungalow and pushed aside floor-length drapes revealing a panoramic view of a waterhole and wide grassy plains. In the distance, a herd of gazelle grazed peacefully.

Barrister Stanley didn't care what the cost; you couldn't buy this feeling in England. He enjoyed luxury. This setting would impress even a dead-beat son. The environment encouraged philosophical discussions; discovering the meaning of life together, father and son. The boy would learn to love him, to respect him, perhaps even request his company after this time together in the so called cradle of civilization.

He thought of his own father with whom he spent memorable, meaningful days and hours as a young boy and as a young man. He remembered their talks, walking along the road or sitting at the kitchen table on cold winter evenings. He wanted the talks to linger, sometimes to avoid going to bed, but also because he loved being with his father.

Now, as an adult, the barrister didn't have time. He couldn't remember ever sitting around the kitchen table after a meal or between meals. His wife stopped asking him to perform menial repairs around the house because she understood his commitment to his clients. He was late at the office more often than he was home for dinner. It was easy as a boy, with his father. Why was it difficult for him now, as a parent? What was it with his son? There was always tension. Conversations were confrontations.

Andrew stood at the window of the *banda* looking beyond the plains. He didn't want to be here. Usually he could avoid his father, but even his mother wanted him to make this safari. They would have such a wonderful time together. She wished she could come. If she wished it, why didn't she do it? *He* didn't wish it. She, they, both parents gave him no choice. Oh well, he shrugged his shoulders to no one in particular and slumped into a large chair, dangling one leg over the arm.

"Ah! Here we are, Andrew...... Africa......" The words lingered as he let the dream sink in. "Let's unpack and go to the lodge to meet some of the other chaps." He ran his fingers through his thick head of hair. "What do you say? I'm ready for a pint, how 'bout you?" They could have a beer or two together now; they were men-on-safari.

"Yeah. You go ahead. I'll just unpack 'n shower. Catch ya later?"

This was not starting off the way the father hoped, but he wasn't going to let the boy put a damper on the trip and he headed off, back down the foot path, past the gift shop and into the buzzing lodge.

Andrew sat on the veranda chewing on ice from a tall, frosted Coke. He ordered room service. Why not? "This was Africa." Already it was dusk and his father was not back. He looked across the waterhole. As the sun started to slip, impala grazed along the shore.

Below the verandah, huge hippos yawned and stretched and played in the water. The mother nudged and pushed the baby for encouragement. With no neck, she arched, thrusting her head backward, parallel to her backside, displaying an unexpected flexibility of the spinal cord. Her gaping mouth revealed long teeth which ringed the perimeter of the upper and lower jaws.

Andrew snatched another Coke from the mini-bar and slunk into a leather deck chair to watch. The family of hippos frolicked in the water, their huge bodies splashed, blew, and snorted in the twilight. Eventually, the mother nudged the baby toward the shore in front of the thatched *banda*. Slowly, playfully they made their way to the shoreline and emerged one step at a time, one heavy leg in front of the other.

The sun continued its descent. On the opposite bank, a large crocodile dropped underwater. Only its eyes protruded as black, floating golf balls, which broke the surface of the water forming a triangle with the nostrils.

Ashore, the beached mushrooms snorted and foraged the dry, parched land finding nourishment. Together the mother and baby walked: silently with deliberation. The infant satisfied, gracefully plodded, one step at a time, back into the water, submerged and was no longer seen. The mother soon followed.

A family of warthogs walked directly in front of where he sat. Warthogs. An appropriate name, he thought. Both words conjured up ugly images. Warts. Hogs. Bristly whiskers protruded along each side of the snout from beneath stubby horns. Stunted legs supported a barrel body, and the hogs carried their tails upright like communications antennae. He found them repugnant. The warthogs rooted for grubs in the shallow, dry dirt then strutted single file, their babies following in mock prissiness across the path, across the plains, down the dusty trail into the brush; unabashedly arrogant. He disliked them. He brought out his sketch pad before he completed his thoughts and sketched these warts, these hogs. His hand worked quickly as he roughed-out the prissy pigs, marching in procession across his page.

He looked up at the now mauve sky and held his breath. Nine, he counted. Nine elephants moved toward the waterhole. One was so large his belly hung to his ankles. The mammoths did not go directly to the water. The large bull dusted himself with dirt using his long trunk to throw the cool earth. He lobbed the clay overhead. Reaching for another snout-full he dusted one side of his frame blowing the fine sand through his long proboscis. His trunk swung freely and limp like an oversized fire hose as he tossed the cool dirt deliberately at each part of his massive anatomy, finally throwing the soft dust between his front legs onto his low slung belly.

The rest of the pachyderms lumbered toward the *bandas*. The herd regrouped for a caucus. In a circle, then as a rounded pod, they marched toward the water. The first two reached the shoreline to drink. The others followed. Finally the last two juveniles played tug-o-war, their trunks entwined as they pulled one direction, backing up, then pulled in the other direction giving way.

Andrew looked up from his sketch pad. Zebra trotted in like thoroughbreds without jockeys. Eight or ten came to the water's edge. The skittish zebra satisfied their thirst and moved on. Two gazelle engaged in playful chase 'round and around further down the meadow. The elephant continued to drink. Andrew remembered reading that like the camel, elephants store water needing to drink every two days. Their thirst quenched, they moved off in single file. The last two adolescent elephant, facing-off, played back and forth gently pushing and shoving, head butting and trunk twisting, lingering behind as the herd lumbered off.

A single, lone elephant now came from the far side of the clearing. He acknowledged the playful juveniles then moved on along the shoreline to drink. The young elephant continued to tussle, and crashed through the trees finally walking side by side until no longer in view. The straggler walked the length of the waterhole stopping to pause in the darkness. He lingered. No other animals remained. Finally, the outsider meandered off. The old bull did not take the path of the herd. He took the route of a drifter and padded to the forest in silence.

Birds quieted in the tree tops, gazelle bedded for the night.

Andrew reflected: perhaps this was the essence of Africa, the peaceful partaking of the waterhole, herds sharing the land and the environment, and doing so with a simple beauty uninterrupted and uncluttered. The irony of it occurred to him, his father at his own watering hole.

* * *

In the morning Andrew and his father headed out in an open lorry; the fine red dust billowed; it covered and clung to their skin, it clogged their pores. The entourage included the guide, who later carried a gun, Andrew and his father, and a second gunman. They came upon a tall, red termite hill. The four meter mound was smoothed and ringed with dried elephant dung. "It's an elephant sleeping ground," the guide explained.

"Elephant sleep only a few hours in the coolest part of the night." He turned around to face them in the back seat, "They lean against the gentle slope of the hill, are immediately asleep and snore very loudly through their long trunks." The vehicle vibrated as it idled. "If they need water before they get up, they reach inside their mouths, draw up a source and disperse it on their glands." Wisps of premature grey protruded from under the guide's ranger hat; Andrew respected his training and knowledge. "It is speculated," he continued, "that they have a separate sack or pouch for storing water inside the stomach or adjacent to it, though this has not been confirmed by autopsy. They are also able to regurgitate the water when they need it," he concluded as they drove on.

The guide was one of the directors of the lodge and a well-known, seasoned and respected game warden. He agreed to take the British client and his son because of their expressed interest in the ecosystem. They paid a great deal of money for this personally guided photographic safari. The money they paid assisted environmental causes, especially related to the protection of endangered animals.

The mission was a dangerous one. The client wanted to track and photograph rhinoceros. The rhino, nearly extinct, topped the endangered species list for over fifteen years, with little hope of protection. Governments tried various methods of intervention, protection and punishment in different countries, but the poachers seemed to win. The sale of rhino horn, used as an aphrodisiac, made wealthy men of illegal hunters.

To locate the elusive beast, they drove deep into the bush. They bounced along on the track, the father vocal about each observation. "Good Lord! Do you see it, Andrew?" he said turning toward his son. "Look at the legs on those ostrich! They are running as fast as we are driving! Good Lord, lad!"

Andrew looked, he saw, he observed. He said nothing.

They turned off the track on a narrow path, barely wide enough for the vehicle. Alongside the path a small pack of female elephant and several young were making their way. The driver stopped the dusty lorry. There were two very young calves, one perhaps three weeks, the guide indicated. The baby was not developmentally able to use its trunk to much advantage. Yet it still tried to grasp the grass by twisting its tiny trunk around a clump of green, pulling the clump from its roots and pushing the small bundle up to its mouth. Supporting his little trunk with his front leg, and with great effort, the baby lifted the proboscis, grass and all, to his mouth. The client, by now, hauled every lens out of the case and he clicked with great abandon. "Capital!" he whispered, reaching for another lens. "Just capital! It's brilliant, Andrew! "

Andrew was spellbound by the scene, and he realized that he and his father responded very differently.

They drove deep into the bush until they ran out of road. The rest of the safari would be on foot as they tried to locate the reclusive rhinoceros. As they disembarked, they looked around the truck; they saw nothing. The barrister was prepared with camera gear hanging from his neck and both arms, the straps crisscrossing his chest. Andrew had a camera as well, in his pocket. The other men carried rifles in the ready position.

Without instruction, they knew to make not a sound. They knew to avoid stepping on a twig or branch and to stifle any cough. They did not breathe as they walked, sometimes crouched, following the lead of the guide. The gunman followed in the rear. They walked single file deep into the thick underbrush. In some places the forest was so dense, they lost the sunlight.

The leaves rustled. The guide stopped short. Andrew, third in line after his father, flinched and halted. He knew the loud beat of his pulse tipped-off some unknown creature: the rhino. They stood frozen. His heart pounded. The palms of his hands dripped. He wiped them against his pant legs. What was he doing here, just so that his father could take photos of a rhinoceros? The trip suddenly seemed more absurd and outrageous than it had in the planning stages. Perspiration dripped into his eye brows and down his temples. And then, after interminable seconds, as if in total control, guinea fowl scratched and scampered into view. Merely guinea fowl, followed by an inaudible sigh from the group.

They walked on through the thick bush in collective silence until they came to a clearing where gazelle grazed. The guide offered a few words of instruction as they sat at the edge of the meadow. Yesterday, by helicopter, he spotted the rhino on the other side of the clearing. They were getting close now. There were two and they would not go far in one day. The success of the mission, and the safety of all, depended on their communal efforts. They must all be vigilant. They must watch in all directions. Rhino were skittish. Their eyesight was poorly developed, but their sense of hearing was acute. The stalkers would be heard before they were ever in sight of the prehistoric beasts. Rhinos charged blindly. The trackers would have no chance.

What they must do, the ranger instructed, was locate the animals, circle behind the pair, get into position to make the photographs, then leave quickly, and he emphasized this point: in total silence, unnoticed. The guide reminded himself that the lawyer and his quiet son paid thousands of pounds for this opportunity, and he knew they must be satisfied with the venture. He also knew that with any irregularity things could go very wrong.

Moving back into the bush, away from the clearing, they continued the search. They all breathed normally while sitting near the opening but back inside the dense bush, Andrew and his father both began sweating profusely. They shook with anticipation and terror, the adrenalin rushed through their collective bodies like water over the Falls. The party scanned what they could see between the leaves and branches in front, in back and to the sides in anticipation and readiness. They remained mute and terrified to breathe aloud.

Through his fear, Andrew thought about his father. He thought about why, as his son, he was here, in dread and fear for his life. He thought of his mother and how she wanted him to come. He wished she were here. He could talk to her sometimes. Not often, and not for too long, but he could...

Suddenly, and without warning, the female lunged at them, her huge ears flapping, trunk raised in deafening trumpet. The guide shouted and yelled, waving his arms frantically; she did not yield, and exposed her vulnerable young calf. The party froze with terror. Again and again, the guide and the gunman tried to distract the elephant as she threatened to charge.

Experienced in the wild, the men from the lodge yelled and bluffed their own aggressive behavior. Andrew and his father yelled from fright as tears streamed down Andrew's face. He simultaneously leaped waving his arms and crouched, doubled over, anticipating the end of life. The mammal was not bluffing and ran full stride toward them. The guide and gunman readied their guns. To put down an elephant was illegal; a female with calf especially traumatic. She lunged within meters of where they stood. Two more giant steps. She was protective and unrelenting. They had no choice. The gunman fired a swift and accurate shot between the eyes directly into the brain. The mammal dropped hard and fast. They ran to get out of her way as she crashed to the ground falling on one knee then dropping to her side.

As they backed away from the horrid sight in shock and trembling, a second female came at them from the side, again full stride in their direction. The guide yelled and waved his arms in a threatening manner. The distraught elephant, ears flapping and upraised trunk bleating in uncontrollable hysteria, charged closer. Again they all yelled and shouted. This time, they were successful in deterring the charge. She backed slowly away, protectively swaying between the murderers and the calf, as she moved back into the thick undergrowth. The silence was deafening. The ground was soaked in dark, red blood, their shoes stained with the extinct life. The only sounds were the uncontrolled, muffled sobs from Andrew.

They drove, in silence, directly to headquarters to report the accident and to take the warden to the scene, describing exactly what happened, then back to the offices to complete all of the paperwork. Because their guide was well known, officials knew the account to be authentic.

When Andrew and his father returned to the *banda* that evening, the father and son did not speak. Each deep in thought, each trying to make sense of the futile day. When they showered the red dust from their hair and skin, and washed the blood from their shoes, they walked, still in silence, to the outdoor dining area. The buffet was heavy, bulky curries, casseroles and grilled meats. They picked at the food; neither of them ate.

How would they tell anyone what had happened? Who could possibly understand? What would he tell his mother? He still wished she were there. In some ways it seemed his father didn't care about what happened. He said nothing. He wondered if his father would amplify the story with each telling, like some do with fishing tales. How could his father be so callous, he wondered?

Late into the night Andrew sketched. He drew the elephant from every angle. He captured the terror in the eyes of the cow as she lifted her trunk in trumpet. He sketched the calf, dependent upon its mother. He sketched the elephants at the water hole. Finally, as the sun rose, he could sketch no more. He put away the pencils and walked past the barrister's room. His father sat on the edge of the bed, his head in his hands. He had not been asleep.

Surprisingly, Andrew felt drawn to the older man. "Father?" he whispered. The man looked up, through red, swollen eyes.

"I'm sorry, Son."

"I'm sorry too, Father. I'm glad Mum's not here this time."

They sat for some moments on the edge of the bed. For the first time, Father said, "You have been drawing. I would like to see your work." He looked directly at his son. "Could I see your sketches, Andrew?"

The Great Zambezi

"Welcome to Victoria Falls. We are pleased that you will be joining us on the river trip today."

It must have been a spontaneous decision. With time to think about it, I would never have gone. Daryle grabbed two hot coffees, I snatched two cold yogurts from the outdoor kiosk and we walked toward the group.

At the booking office people stood around in small groups of twos and threes. By the end of the trip we would be best of friends, exchanging contacts and cards, as often happens in group efforts, especially where survival is involved. Perfect strangers become united in an earthquake, a flood, a neighbourhood fire. No doubt the same would occur here, though in the beginning everyone sized each other up.

Dressing in the morning, I pushed my hair around and glanced in the mirror while listening to the Voice of America morning news report.

The VOA reported that Bill Clinton was nominated at the democratic convention. John Sununu noted that last year Bush was celebrating victory over Iraq stating, "Bush, step aside. You have had your chance." Clinton said, "We can do it."

Around a hundred rafters waited at the office, spilling into the street. We were divided into smaller rafting groups and paired off as sister crafts manned by Western oarsmen Tex and Zimbabwean oarsman Tmombe.

I was sure everyone would be under the age of twenty-five. In fact, from our group there was a family from South Africa, a father and two sons; a German girl, fifteen; two Peace Corps Volunteers from Malawi; a young Frenchman completing his national service headed back to France. His dilemma: what to do, what next, maybe ecology or environment. One Peace Corps teacher expressed frustration with Peace Corps, not the bureaucracy, but the fact that the college students in Malawi didn't want to learn.

A strapping surfer-type wore an earring and pulled his hair into a ponytail. Three others spoke German, and two cow-folks added to the diversity. The cow-girl sported downscale long shorts, her white legs muscular, strong and fit, but waaay too white. She donned wire frame glasses and a pink baseball cap. Her partner wore the cowboy hat and khaki shorts. His skinny legs stuck like broomsticks in sockless tennis shoes. There was also a quiet one. Nervous and alone, he looked like Paulo Rebiero, the brilliant Portuguese doctor. Maybe he was Portuguese. If so, he was a Rebiero. Silent. Didn't speak. Couldn't tell his dialect or language.

As we waited, local kids roamed the streets trying to off-load worthless Zimbabwean dollars. It seemed a friendly culture; everyone appeared to know everyone. They greeted in warm, genuine friendship. Handshakes, enormous smiles, holding hands for the duration of the greeting, men with men, women with women, girls with girls, girls with guys, very warm communication. An attractive man, physically fit, wore a muscle shirt, and well pressed, pleated khaki knee shorts. In the local language, he spoke a long time to a female passerby; animated, kind, gentle, joyous. She left to go on to her job; he stayed. He must be with the river trip.

Someone handed out forms. Digging around for pens, we filled out the papers which released the white water rafting company from any responsibility or accountability for injury, loss, damage or death. In no way would the firm be responsible for any fatality occurring during this trip. These words and signatures set a solemn tone as we planned for this departure from reality, this departure from the shore, this departure on the rafts of the great river Zambezi. Everyone listened with a silent soberness to all words spoken. There was no horseplay, no nervous giggling, no foolishness. Each person took the instructions seriously.

"Welcome to Victoria Falls." The man of the well pressed khaki shorts greeted us. "The great Zambezi starts in central Africa and reaches its pinnacle in the great, tumultuous, thunderous Victoria Falls. At the base of the falls, the river continues to flow through deep gorges and African savannah and finally empties into the Indian Ocean. We are going to travel through rapids four through twenty-one today, stopping at number 11 for a lunch break."

We jumped in the back of an open-sided lorry and bounced along. Still no one spoke to anyone outside their own small group.

We walked to a spot behind the Victoria Falls Hotel where the life jackets were arranged in three piles. The spokesman explained each style and type of vest and the three were rather different.

"Some are made in South Africa, some in China and some are made for the America Cup in the US." He scanned the group then continued. "Each has a slightly different feature." He looked down at the vests. "The most important thing is that they must be tied very tight because," he seemed to look me directly in the eye, "in the unlikely event that someone ends up in the water, it is everyone's responsibility to pull that person back into the raft." He delivered the punch line, "When one grabs the vest, if it falls off because it is not tied tight, you will save the jacket and not the person."

We carefully selected our vests and synched each other up like geishas wrapping our obis tighter and tighter until we breathed with difficulty. One by one we began the steep, long decent down the narrow trail through the gorge to the river.

Carved steps and a few tremulous branches helped one gain footing. Ropes strung along the rock side of the escarpment wall provided a grip where there was nothing else to grasp. A foot trestle, a foot bridge, swaying and wet, included minimalistic rope banisters. Don't look down. Look forward, but not down. We maneuvered across one section of the gorge on to the rocks. Then groped and tip-toed our way over wet, slippery moss, jagged rocks and fast moving gravel down to the roaring river, rock by stone, by rock, sometimes on all fours, at last to the water's edge.

Down the gorge, hollering all the way, leaping gingerly, where we had just crawled and groped, the oarsmen, loud, rowdy and enthusiastic, sprinted to the mighty river.

Once on level ground we regrouped on the edge of a quiet pool for instruction on rafting safety. A tiny crocodile, no more than 15 inches long, nestled among the rocks, probably caught in a rapid and washed to shore, separated from its mother. Tmombe talked to us about when the raft flips over.

"It doesn't matter if it is the crew's fault or the oarsman's fault. Help people get back into the raft. If the raft flips," I sucked in air as he continued, "grab hold of the rope in the centre of the boat. There will be an air pocket.

"Don't panic," he sternly advised. "Let someone know you are there because the oarsman will be trying to account for everyone." Oh. My. God.

"And don't stay there forever. Make your way to the surface," I had difficulty processing this, "and when the boat is righted, climb in and help other crew members." He was right, of course.

"We can never sit back and say, 'Well, I'm okay.' Not until everyone is into the boat and accounted for." Tmombe continued, "If you are tossed out of the raft, stay in the centre of the river." Already I strategized to go to the edge and get out of the pounding water. "This is to avoid the crocodiles who linger on the banks." My head pounded again. "Someone will pick you up. Just stay afloat with your life jacket."

We climbed into the rafts like leggy dancers before a performance and floated about the calm cove. The boat bobbed a bit but remained stable, as we adjusted our postures.

In another raft people executed some sort of game. Probably to keep everyone happy until we launched. It looked like "Simon Says" as they jumped from one side of the raft to the other. They jumped around the raft on command of the oarsman. As we floated around in the current and drifted toward them, I realized they were practicing some drills, some commands relative to craft safety or operations.

We were positioned in the craft according to weight. The heavy persons took the bow, the light ones sat in the rear. I qualified for the back of the bus. Daryle wanted to be by-my-side and arranged to be in the back also.

The other members of our crew turned out to be the long-haired, broad-shouldered, muscular surfer-guy, the Peace Corps Volunteers, he being a brawny, twenty-something strapping American, the Frenchman ending his National Service and the nervous, quiet one who turned out to also be French. They all took the forward positions.

One of them asked the oarsman, as we all realized other crews were practicing regimented drills, "Should we be doing that? Is that what we should do?" He voiced what we all believed, "We are receiving no instruction."

Tex, the *mzungu,* the western oarsman, told us that he did not particularly agree with those techniques. "Sometimes the heavy thrusting can cause the boat to capsize."

"This is what we should do:" We all leaned in convinced our lives were at stake by doing this correctly. "When a wave is coming head on, the oarsman will shout a command. The ones in the front will stand, facing the wave, then lie on the front of the boat to force the weight into the wave." I was tense and relieved to not be in the front.

"The ones in the back must crouch down to keep the boat steady." I could do that. It was apparent that the crew had a lot to do with navigating the craft. There were no passengers on this trip. Every person was a working member of the team and the safety of all depended upon the care and seriousness of the mariners.

The Launch

We launched on the great Zambezi River. Our red raft hugged the rocks at the edge of deep pools. Within minutes the boat thrashed through the first rapids. We clung, white knuckled, to the guideline in the back, Daryle and I hunkered in the stern.

Ice-cold, freezing whitewater lashed and swamped us. Pushed from behind by the power of the water, the force nearly threw me out the far side of the boat. Somehow, I stayed inside the crimson craft.

And this was the first rapid.

With dread I faced the rest of the river trip, counting down the rapids and the hours, knowing that if I lived through this it would be about three in the afternoon when we returned to dry land. I swallowed liters of river water. It was fast; it was powerful. The waves came from all directions as the raft spun and slammed over and under the water.

We managed this test-run, as did the oarsmen, with 'great

skill.' I caught my breath for a brief pause as we drifted with the current toward the next approaching rapid. Daryle said nothing; who could talk? I looked around the raft making eye contact with no one; everyone focused on the river. I froze, soaked through, wet hair glued to my head which protruded through the top of my maize-coloured life preserver like the first daffodil of spring.

"The life vests each have a crescent shaped pillow attached to the back, behind the neck. If you are thrown overboard, lie on your back, extend your legs, put your head back on the headrest pillow and drift with the current. Someone will pick you up." Great.

We drifted toward the next rapid; the oarsman explained how to make the approach.

"Okay, guys," I ignored his gender reference, "on this rapid the waves come in from the front." He yelled over his shoulder. "We have to take this one *broadside*. This will spin the raft," he roared, "and we'll take the following set *backwards*." He shouted the commands gripping his oar with both hands, utilizing the full strength of his arms.

This demanded a reversal in the procedures for the crew. Those of us in the back were now responsible for maintaining the stability of the craft. This meant: lie across the front of the bow, full body weight, hoping to counter-balance the waves and keep the craft afloat until we spun around in the rollers to a frontward position. Gawd, it was scary. Not only did I fear for my life, but my body throbbed with cold tension, and stiffened from the arctic water; and now I had responsibility for the rest of the crew.

We approached the rapids and executed the whitewater exactly as expounded in the strategy, yelling out our stressors. The water thundered yet I heard the others shout. Every time I opened my mouth to scream it filled with water: slow learner. I swallowed much of the river, I don't know how many times completely submerged by the great Zambezi, until I lost both contact lenses.

I blinked my eyes like a flirtatious diva, more like a waterlogged Raggedy Ann. Perhaps the lenses were lost in my eyelids or in the corners of my eyes. Maybe I just lost one. Puleeeeze, I said to the sky. I saw nothing but blurred images. My life was now in danger. I could not see the approaching waves to know how to plan the survival scheme. I closed one eye. No contact. Closed the other. Surely I had not lost both lenses. No vision.

I needed to adjust. My eyes needed to self-correct. I could not see. After about ten minutes, and before the next set of rapids, both lenses popped into focus. They were indeed lodged somewhere inside my eye sockets. What a blessing to have sight.

I think.

Maybe.

At one point I was so terrified I decided I would shut my eyes and just pray for it to be over. In nano-seconds of that choice, I realized I had to be able to see. There was no way I could not know or anticipate, what was coming next.

Tex explained the next set of rapids and the tactic. We watched in horror as our companion raft flipped, tossing the crew into the roaring waters. Without having time to dwell on their disaster and misfortune, the rapid was upon us. Terrified again, we got through it upright. There was a lot of hooting and jubilant hollering between the oarsmen. The only hollering coming from me was the African pounding of my pulse.

We picked up the young cow-girl who made her way to the edge of the river, still floating in the deep river water, but clinging to the massive rocks along the water's edge. We hauled her aboard by her vest. She was shaken, but not panicked, happy that her metal framed glasses stayed with her, attached by a pink croaky chord. Holding on as tight as she could, she was still thrown out. She lost her pink baseball cap.

Further downstream, the young boy floated in the middle of the river, not at all panicked. He did exactly the right thing, lying on his back, legs extended, waiting for a pick up. We hauled him into the back of the raft and drifted to a quiet place at the side of the roaring river.

When we stopped for lunch at a shaded picnic site the young German girl told me she was thrown from the raft twice. The raft capsized pulling her underneath. She swallowed a lot of water and came up under the boat in the air pocket and caught a breath.

She was immediately pulled down by the force of the water. In broken English she said, "I could not get up. I panicked under the water." She gasped for air as she spoke and took a swig at her coke. "I had no air. I knew I was panicked and that scared me more."

"Do you remember getting back into the boat?" I asked. "Were you thrown free?" She said the raft was finally up-righted and she was pulled back inside. She took a bite of her salami and cheese sandwich. "Would you do it again?" I asked. She paused a long time and looked out at the river.

"Tomorrow? Definitely not tomorrow." She looked back at me, "Perhaps another year, perhaps later."

Back on the river, as we waited in the calm, an eight foot crocodile also waited on a sunny rock. Someone asked what we were all thinking, "How can you risk having rafters flip out and float the current of the river, waiting to be picked up?" Answer: The crocs are not swimming in the whitewater. They are only in the calm pools. Rafters will always be picked up in the quiet pools. That's the answer?

As a second raft approached, two floaters bobbing on the Great Zambezi in their yellow life vests, slithered, cold and exhausted, into their own raft, but not before the young boy told me he was South African on winter break with one more year for his O-Levels.

The next rapids were the longest of the lot. While not necessarily more powerful, they were much longer and if you were thrown, you would have a rougher trip down the river because of the turbulent water. I clutched the guide rope until my knuckles protruded through my now translucent iris flesh. I did not want to crash through the rapids on a solo flight.

The approach was again explained by the strapping oarsmen who faced us, their backs to the upcoming whitewater, as they shouted the strategic plan to both crews.

We would make the approach, do this, do that, depending upon how the waves broke. Everything went just about as anticipated. I clutched the guide rope at the back of the raft.

Then, the force of the water was so great my whole body

lifted and flew from the side of the craft into the swirling current. Still clinging to the rope like a mountaineer grips rappelling ropes, I held the line though completely submerged, propelled off the side of the boat.

Survival thoughts rocked through my mind at flash-speed: If I let go, I'm crashing through this long stretch of rapids alone and I am going to freeze solid like an oversized purple Popsicle just before I'm completely bashed and battered. If I don't let go, I will not have any air to breathe and I will have to breathe-in all this water like an enema through my nose.

Within seconds, before I blacked out, the oarsman looked back, saw me in the water, dropped the oars, hoisted me back into the boat, re-grasped the oars, re-gained control of the raft, maneuvered us through the rest of the long rapids and everyone maintained their positions, including me, through the remainder of the white water.

The two burly men in the front, the surfer-guy and the Peace Corps guy, also flew out during part of that run, though neither was thrown far from the raft. When in calm water again, I thanked the oarsman for hauling me aboard.

"Man, never seen anyone do a back flip off the raft before. Awesome."

How he managed that, standing during the rowing, taking time to reach down over the side to haul me in, regain control with the oars through the remainder of that rapid, I will never comprehend.

Awesome.

Smoke That Thunders
Mosi-oa-Tunya

My head ached in the rush of the moment. I was sure to have a pounding, throbbing headache the rest of the day. How could it hurt so much so fast? My contacts cleared quickly; my jawbone clenched in an unrelenting bite as I ground my teeth to stubs, leaving a corrugated washboard of my lower jaw.

The grip I maintained on the guide rope did not loosen. The tension lingered like a recently scorned woman. Sweating. Pounding. Throbbing. At last we were through the plundering, merciless white foam.

Tex and Tmombe, the oarsmen, hollered simultaneously, "Everybody out. This one's too rough." Impassable. The next rapid frothed, spit venom and defied access, necessitating *portage*. We hoisted the rafts out of the water and made our way over the rocks. At one point we clutched a rope, attached to the escarpment like a horizontal rappel.

The bank proved slippery and wet. The view over my shoulder, down to the river, was of a deep cavern. The water, wild and ferocious, surged through the cleavage. We were not going through Smoke That Thunders. We were not rafting that one: Impassable.

The next cascade of water emulated a mini falls, thunderous and spectacular. As we approached large boulders on the bank of the river, we realized the oarsmen intended to shoot this rapid solo. We leaned against the smooth wet stones and watched. Standing at the head of the raft, they plunged into the fullness of the rapid. Their oars flashed like the batons of a majorette, the rafts balanced precariously on end. The boats contorted, twisted, tossed and turned like hot kernels of popped corn.

Through practiced determination and skill, both boats made it through to the hearty applause and rowdy hoots and yowls of ecstasy. Still trembling from cold, we re-boarded our red raft and continued downstream toward the next rapid. How many more? How much longer this joy ride?

A group of young boys yelled from the banks of the river, fishing poles in hand. The oarsman waved and the boys jumped up and down waving with both arms, rods dangling aimlessly.

"These are some of my favourite kids," Tex told us. "The one in the front is an all-time treasure. I see these kids every day." He plunged his paddle deep. "They always have a greeting for me."

"Hey, Tex," we discerned. The water was too loud to hear words. The young boys ran to the river's edge to watch the rafts crash the rapids. They shouted to the oarsmen, possibly thinking, 'I will be an oarsman. I will ride the mighty rapids of the Great Zambezi.'

"On my day off," he swiveled to talk to us, "I sometimes bring my kayak across the river, paddle over and talk to these boys." We splashed through a calm stretch. The blue-black colour of the deep river contrasted with the very white frothy waves. "They idolize the oarsmen. They dream that one day they will be the same. But they don't go to school," he shouted with anger and disappointment.

"I talk to them; they seem clever and they should have a chance for education," he said still paddling down river. "I keep talking to them about going to school, in order to become whatever they want to become in life." He waved at them again as we roared past. "They can get jobs, work the river, work in shops, but only if they go to class." Maybe the oarsman will impose some influence. I wondered about his opportunity, Tex, the *mzungu*. Would he be influential or insignificant?

Through the whole river voyage I alternated between fear and panic like Thor Heyerdahl on the *Kon Tiki*.

A huge wave approaches: Breath stops. Heart stops. The skin over my knuckles is blue-thin from the grip, clenching the guide rope of the raft. The wave, bigger and bigger washes over. It crashes with enormous speed; it crashes with enormous roar and thunder overhead, body and raft.

Hold breath,
    close eyes,
        close mouth.
            Don't take in water, it's all too fast.

The water crashed-walloped over and into every bodily opening, mouth, eyes, ears, nose. I swallowed much water; I thought I might be sick.

When we finally navigated through the final rapid, I realized there was no relief. Yes, we were on dry land. Dry land at the bottom of the ravine. The only way out was the compulsory, obligatory climb up the wall of the gorge.

Daryle preceded me as we climbed the sheer cliff, up the stair steps, clustered one hundred at a group, at a steep incline. Wet: wet soil, wet stairs, wet arms, legs and body, wet hair, everything was wet but the bright sky.

The strength in my legs vanished; they refused to work. "I can't make my legs work; they're like putty," I breathed to Daryle. The only way I managed to climb the steps up the escarpment, step by step, was to lift and push my thighs into place. To move upward, up the narrow, steep steps I reached under my knee to hoist my leg placing it on the next upward step. First right, then left. I felt a helpless loss of control.

Daryle grabbed my arm to pull me the final steps up the gorge. The extreme incline, difficult to manage, was surpassed only by the horrible stairs. With agonizing effort I made my way to the top where others sat drinking cold drinks in the open truck. Graciously, they said, "Hey, take your time. We're glad for the rest."

Every muscle and sinew I ever learned the name of gave me pain.
My muscles hurt where I didn't know there were any.
I burned where I didn't know there was tissue at all.
Even the tendons around my ankles stretched out of whack.

My biceps felt overextended like rubber bands pulled taut, ready to snap. My legs moved like bungee cords, bunging all over the place unattached, out of control. My thighs ached with every step, my calves, spared only somewhat by comparison. I negotiated each step at impossibly slow pace with embedded agony. Deep breathing hurt my whole chest cavity as well as my back muscles.

How did this happen? The arduous hike down the cliff to the river? The horrific trudge along the Zambezi climbing over wet boulders and slippery rocks? The punishing slog back up the escarpment one hundred steps at a time? Perhaps. But primarily I thought the pain came from the physical tension and angst garnered from the stress of the river, of the rapids, of the whitewater.

A hot shower, shampoo and two aspirin helped soothe and warm the body. A stiff gin-tonic helped too. The headache never materialized, but my legs remained like rubber, like silly-putty with no form or shape. At seven we shuffled across the street to look at promised photos from the day. While I dreaded even that short walk, curiosity spurred me on to see what kind of pictures they produced.

Drawn to the outside disco rock-n-roll sounds, we found oarsmen and crew sitting in bleachers and at tables with beer and drinks watching an outdoor oversized TV monitor. It displayed an outrageous video of whitewater rafting. The music rocked incompatible with the drum of reggae Zimbabwean music. The oarsmen in the bleachers relived and hooted each rapid, and sang the lyrics to the rock-n-roll like fans at a soccer match. The extreme video was of *today's* river trip.

Two rows in front of us I noticed the cow-girl; a new baseball cap replaced her submerged pink beanie. She sat alongside her partner who sang with passion like a famous rocker, a cross between Buddy Holly with *Peggy Sue* and Bill Haley *Rockin' Around the Clock*. I looked for the surfer-dude from our crew, but was distracted by the powerful video. The young German girl, fifteen now going on twenty-two, swaggered with a cigarette dangling from the edge of her mouth. The group grew in size including most of the rafters from today's trip, about one-hundred, plus the oarsmen and other long-hair types.

Two shaggy kayakers made their way through the rapids, defied death, perched themselves precariously on tree branches, dangled over boulders and shot stills with expensive camera equipment and high speed film.

There was much enthusiasm over each rapid, which proved to be outrageously contagious. The video camera-guy, tall and lanky, sported the prerequisite stringy hair: a genius who controlled the river while running the video camera.

To see the rapids one by one in the film terrified me. To go through them was one thing, but I didn't see their power at the time. The video proved awe-some, awe-full, in the original sense of the words. After twenty minutes, the photographers set up their boards for a display of photos. They captured several still shots of each raft showing the crew in various positions at different rapids. The camera never lies.

Kayakers in the role of cinematographers captured us on video through, under and over the rapids. There we were, in the back of our raft. Not brave as macho accessories to the crew, which we felt we were. They exposed us, shriveled in the stern as commanded. Of course we ordered a set of photos and the living colour video. No bravado. No machismo. Just hunkered down, controlling the back of the little red raft.

Awesome.

Hakuna Matata

Jambo! That's tourist-talk in Kenya, Kiswahili for Hey! Yo! Wassup! Of course when Kenyans greet each other it's much more complicated and lengthy but we tourists like *Jambo!* It's punchy and has an edge to it.

The car, a white Suzuki Safari, long wheel base, loaded like a *haji* truck headed to Mecca. We accrued so much rental gear for the small space it took over an hour to inventory, pack and re-pack. We made a complete log: 4 forks, 4 spoons, 2 sharp knives, a ladle, spatula, frypan, 2 sauce pans, a basin, water container, jerry can for gaz, a useless, warped, sagging, bent plywood table with folding metal legs, four rusty camp chairs, two wobbly tents, two blankets.

It was Jen's first trip to Africa, Jen, our daughter-in-law, Ian's wife. Ian and his sister bounced around east and north Africa, central Africa and southern Africa since they were kids. I think we all subconsciously hoped Jen would catch the fire; catch the obsession we felt for the continent: the big sky, the solitude, the intimacy with the universe.

Jen was gifted to our family. None of us could believe she actually agreed to marry Ian, the kid who never picked up his socks, the kid who stayed up all night completing papers before the due-date even for his doctorate. She was like royalty, like a princess and we reveled over our good fortune.

Ian shoved large foam sleeping mats plus sleeping bags, the wine box, hand carry bags, camera cases and blankets into the back seat. Jen and I sat hugging our knees.

We drove through the city-centre of Nairobi, 'round the roundabouts towards the Tanzanian border. Daryle went inside a small office to deal with local administrivia including visas, paperwork for the car and Tanzanian shillings.

While we waited in the car, Kenyan ladies poked their heads

through the windows to offer us trinkets for our necks, ears and ankles, plus decorated, beaded gourds. When one vendor offered necklaces of carved wooden animals, we told her, sitting in our packed truck, we had no space for anything else. "The pieces are for your neck, not the car," he had a point. We rolled up the windows.

An older man seemed fascinated with Ian's wildlife T-shirt. He read it:

"One earth, One change."

"One Chance," Ian corrected.

"Oh," he replied. Then, "What does that mean, one chance?" He looked at Ian.

"Well," Ian began, "This is our earth and we have to be careful not to destroy it."

"Oh, like eh-co-lagy," he struggled with the pronunciation.

"Yeah, that's it."

"There's lion, ele-pant. What's that big ship?" he asked pointing to Ian's shirt.

"Oh, that's a ram."

"Big ship?"

"Something like that. It's in America."

"Do they ate them?"

"They eat sheep."

"Can I have yo shat? I give you these necklace."

"Oh, thank you, I need the shirt."

"Ferry fine shat. Ah you sho?" He cocked his head.

"Yeah, I need the shirt."

"It's smat, very smat shat."

When Daryle returned, we unlocked the doors and rolled down the windows, eager to be on our way. The starter would not feed gas to the engine. We tried over and over. It seemed there was an air bubble. Afraid of flooding, we tried the choke. The car did not budge. Oodles of bantam boys offered much advice about mechanics. Some said to go back to Kenya, others recommended a mechanic friend in Tanzania.

They filed the distributer points and disconnected the fuel pump hose. Others took turns trying to suck fuel out of the hose.

At one time a car guy said, "Ah, Sir, it's the cah-bah-rae-tah." He removed the whole thing, set it on the ground, on the side of the road and took it apart piece by piece, cleaned off each part, put it back together through sheer street-smarts and hours later carefully placed it under the hood. We got back into the car and hopefully turned the key. Nothing.

We waited. Two army battalions marched by in cadence; no matching uniforms, no socks, beat-up rifles slung over their shoulders. They sang Kiswahili marching tunes in blended harmony between a shouted cadence of Hut, Two, Three, Four.

One mechanic offered to take us to Nairobi then re-plan our trip for us. Another took-over and hours later a Tanzanian car-person tried several voodoo things under the hood. He worked for two hours, no voodoo.

Eventually, a safari guide from Abercrombie & Fitch came over. "Well, I think I know what the issue is," he said leaning in. "You have an ignition security lock." He disconnected the wires, turned the security system off, and turned the key. We held our breath. The car started right up. Plus we now had a clean cah-bah-rae-tah.

We had no choice but to return to Nairobi; the car was unreliable. Frustrated and angry, we phoned Habib's Car Rental and drove the truck back. It was late. It was dark. Habib's son met us and diffused the situation only somewhat by saying he had a rough day too; another of his cars was in an accident. We explained the problems, unloaded the car for a complete checkup and repair and headed into town.

Jen didn't say much. We forced ourselves to find a small meal as we had eaten nothing of substance since our feast the night before at the Nairobi Carnivore, known for wild game and the exotic African meats. During the day there was no time for lunch, having spent hours at the border. The long drive back to Nairobi in the dark was not conducive to stopping in case the car refused to start.

We staggered into the hotel restaurant. The menu was sparse and uninspired. I finally ordered a tenderloin. Big mistake. I should have asked "Tenderloin of what, Sir?" The meat sat like venom in the pit of my stomach. I cramped and heaved and re-gurgitated the entire meal. Between the diarrhea, and cramps from four am, I finally threw up all the red meat, whatever it was. In, up and out. I consumed the box of Lomotil and handfuls of charcoal pills.

It's another day; I'm good-to-go. *Hakuna matata,* no problem.

With the promise that the Suzuki was in great shape, *hakuna matata,* we dashed back to the Tanzanian embassy, filled out more forms, donated more photos, paid more fees and demand-ed the visa stamp be given instantly rather than waiting twenty-four hours. We played the ugly American card.

New visas in hand, we returned to Habib's, repacked the car, checked the starter, took off the security, electrical system. The car started right up.

Again at the Tanzania border the hawkers continued their trade. True, they sold and worked for a living, but it was tire-some. They didn't give up; they didn't let up. But they were not really rude.

"Why don't they leave us alone?" Jen voiced her annoyance. "We have to keep the windows up or they just keep hanging and leaning in." She swiveled away from the vendors. "It's so hot with the windows up." Jen voiced how we all felt.

They offered gourds of all shapes decorated with drawings and cowry shells. They sold shoulder-wide Masaai necklaces made of tiny Japanese glass beads: red, green, white, orange and blue crys-tals strung together on wire in traditional Masaai patterns. Some necklaces featured long strings of beads which hung to the waist-line with shiny tin arrows that jangled with motion. These were tempting. The earrings were small and silly. I knew I could find better samples.

"Look at the *kangas,*" I nudged Jen from inside the sauna.

"Oh, like your table cloths? Your beach wraps?"

Colourful *kanga* cloths hung neatly folded in prints of yellow and brown, yellow and green, blue and white, red and orange. By now I owned stacks of *kangas.* Each cloth is as long as your out-stretched arms and is wide enough to cover a woman from her neck to her knees or from her chest to her toes. They are still sold in pairs.

Kanga comes from the Kiswahili verb *ku-kanga*, to wrap. While I always sifted through stacks of folded cloth looking for colour, *kangas* are known for the sayings, often proverbs printed along the border. I always asked for a translation, and jotted down whatever they told me. My knowledge of Kiswahili was enhanced by safari terms, *tembo*, *twiga*, *simba*, elephant, giraffe, lion, which sometimes danced into the proverbs.

I remembered typical sayings on the *kangas* which included:

We are all passengers, God is the driver.

Everything is all right if you love each other.

Even though I have nothing, I have not given up my desire to get what I want. *This I love.*

I'm afraid of a lion with its strong teeth but not a man with his words. *My favourite.*

* * *

We set up camp at Lake Manyara. The night sounds scared Jen. They were loud and unfamiliar. The hyenas howled, wart hogs snorted and grunted and baboons yelped all night, as if they were right outside our tents. They sounded brash. They were bothersome.

"What's *that*?" The baboons barked louder and louder as the sky darkened. "Where *are* they?" Jen continued. "How close will they *come*?" She continued to fidget in her camp chair.

"Are wart hogs *dangerous*? They're really cute," again from Jen.

"They're disgusting. I hate them," I retorted.

"Why? They're cute the way they go in a line with the little ones following."

"They're prissy; arrogant. I hate the way they swivel their hips, marching along in line, their tails held high like antennae." I also sounded arrogant.

"Awe, I think they're cute."

"At any rate, the pigs won't hurt you, unless they are protecting their young, but they can roust around your food. That's one reason we keep it locked in the car."

"What about the *hyenas*? They sound so *close.*" I sensed a bit of panic.

"They can be a pain in the patoot, those cheeky buggers," I tried to laugh it off. "They snatch food from your containers even when you have lids. It's best to put your food away as soon as you have eaten."

"Then, if you're not careful," Ian added, "they sneak behind your camp chair and lock their jaws around your ankles, burrowing their teeth into your flesh."

"Stop it, Ian." Jen jabbed him with her elbow.

I love the night sounds of Africa, never knowing exactly what they are or who is making them.

It rained all night, a heavy, weighty downpour that did not stop until eight in the morning. It was way too wet for an early morning game drive. When the deluge ended we boiled coffee for the thermos, took down the tents, heavy with water, packed all the wet gear and headed on toward Ngorongoro Crater.

We drove on slick, deeply rutted, muddy roads, through villages and around Masaai compound *bomas*. Warrior-clad Masaai men in red plaid skirts and blood red capes knotted at the neck or over one shoulder stood tall clutching even taller spears. Strands of multicoloured beads encircled their necks, wrists and ankles. They presented themselves handsomely with ears pierced up and down the ridge and lobes; their beads dangled in clanking décor and bounced off each toned, bronze chest.

The traffic slowed as we reached a village where a crowd milled about the street. Some problem or demonstration, but we were forced to drive through it. Slowly making our way through the throng, we saw a child on the edge of the road. His head was bloodied. He was dead. Jen gasped. I gawked. The accident was recent. We were white *mzungu*. We had no choice but to push forward lest we be charged, accused, required to drive, pay, go to prison, be caught in the wrong place, wrong time as a potential crowd gathered and rage grew. The tendency, western logic, our culture screamed, help this child, family, situation. We could not help. The child was dead at the fault of someone else.

The mud, the consistency of thick clay, like *adobe* before it hardens: slippery, that gooey, sticky, clay, like *tsjika*, Ethiopian clay for making bricks. The clay that makes the sound of its name when you step through it. *Tsjika, tsjika, tsjika,* squish, squish, squish.

Keeping a good speed kept us from getting stuck in the adhesive mud. At one point we lost control of the truck, swerving diagonally like a plane in a wind shear, then spinning round and around while oncoming traffic waited for our demise. We hit a puddle of mud which obliterated the view from the windshield. While we grasped for control, the wipers refused to function and we tried to negotiate the road by driving with everyone looking out a side window. Ian yelled from the passenger seat, "Bridge! Bridge! Slow it down." Miraculously we hit the bridge head-on, rather than broadside or missing it all together. *Hakuna matata.*

"Oh my God!"

"I don't believe it!"

"Unbelievable!" We all said at once.

"Are we there yet?" from Jen.

The Elephant in the Room

Toward Ngorongoro the weather calmed. The clouds parted and the sun illuminated the colours of the crater basin. Ngorongoro crater is the world's largest intact, inactive volcanic caldera. It measures 14 miles diameter, 19 kilometers across, and includes a soda/salt lake at the bottom.

At the rim of the depression we picked up a guide and began the horrific switch-back descent. Already squeezed into the Suzuki we squished even further to accommodate the required chaperon. He wedged his fragrant body into the front seat aiming us down the zigzag road. Fortunately the windows were all open but Jen and I sat in the back seat, downwind. We exchanged glances. She pulled at her nose while shifting her eyes from side to side.

Although the road into the crater was dry, it was steep, narrow and one-lane. Daryle edged the tippy truck downward, avoiding the edge of the cliff, clinging to the wall of the caldera. Animals used this path also, though none were on the dusty road as we descended the terrifying trail.

Finally at the bottom of the crater, we drove directly upon five female lions, full bellied, sleeping off yesterday's zebra. We felt compelled to observe the lions, but sleeping lions, gorged sleeping lions, are about as interesting as watching Grandpa snooze on the sofa after a holiday meal. Using four cameras from four windows we shot the obligatory photos, some indecent, spread eagle as they lounged on their backs, then drove on.

During the rains the crater exuded lush shades of green: verdant, olive, jade and khaki blended to create the road to an African Oz.

Zebra grazed along the slopes, their furry young foals mingled with wildebeest and calves who kicked their legs and trotted without care along fast flowing streams. A zebra rested its head on the striped neck of its mate; the classic pose.

"I can't believe I'm here. This is beautiful. I love the zebra," Jen said alternating between the camera lens and natural vision. "I could stay here forever." Above it all, heavy swollen clouds held dark chambers of water.

Thousands of flamingos, like Salvador Dali elephants with colossal bodies and spindly legs, lined the shores of Lake Makat in the pit of the crater. How can feathers make noise, pink such a soft, quiet colour? As they spread massive wings with an expanse of over five feet, I didn't expect the sound of moving feathers as they whooshed by.

Some sat in the shallow water fluttering and bathing like birds in a back yard bird-bath. The colossal colony cackled and honked in a high pitch. For social birds, communication is critical and the numbers made them collectively loud. They screeched like a gymnasium full of teenage girls enraptured by a rock star.

"We have many badhs here. You like badhs? British people love baddhing. There's a medowlahk," the guide tried to be informative. "Up in trees; they-a's a vulcha."

We drove near a few majestic elephant bulls. According to the aromatic guide, only the males came into the crater for a week or so, but it was too hot for them to stay. They came down for the grass then went back up to the top, up the steep, narrow switch backs. Ugly hyena with strong spotted broad shoulders slept in the grass waiting for nocturnal opportunities and someone else's kill. Herds of bearded wildebeest wandered unfazed by the spotted ones in their midst.

Then
>Big lumps on the plains
>>Prehistoric double horns on the dark male
>>>One light female and another dark female
>>>>They stand
>>>>>Take steps near the car
>>>>>>We gasp, they stop
>>>>>>>Eyeing each other
>>>>>>>>Remarkable creatures, now nearly extinct.
>>>>>>>>Three illusive rhino.

We started up the zigzag path on the return to the crater top. Daryle shifted into four wheel drive and we began the climb up the steep grade. The surge of the car caused us to rubber-neck as we bashed forward. My head split from tension and knocking against the top of the vehicle. The wheels could not avoid the crevices, but coming out of the fissures we heaved forward as projectiles with nowhere to go but the roof of the truck.

At the top we offloaded the guide and un-wedged ourselves from our overloaded Suzuki. The spectacular view from the top of the rim made me gasp for air. From the top of the crater we scanned the vast floor of the basin some 2000 feet below. The sun gleamed on the green valley, the game roamed and clouds slowly traversed the sky.

"Whew. I need the loo," I blurted. "*Wapi choo? Choo kiku wapi?* Where's the loo?" I used my tacky Kiswahili since *choo* actually means something like poo. The more polite phrase is *Iko wapi uani?* Where's the out back? *Wapi choo* is easier to remember and tourists aren't always polite; you hear it often.

"Me too," chirped Jen. She was shy and tried to get used to squatting behind a bush.

We unloaded the truck, set up the tents and rusty camp chairs then set up the sagging table to prepare dinner. The critical piece was unpacking the bruised box of cabernet. Once we enjoyed a sip of the red deliverance, poured into our dented tin cups, we started to relax. We cranked open cans of chili. Jen diced up a red onion and I sliced the Emmentaler for condiments.

Anticipating the rain, we completed dinner, packed away the dishes and most of the rickety gear; we were off to the bushes, our own private *choos*, as the first large drops of rain drenched our light jackets. We sprinted to the tents and lounged on the foam mats as we waited for the rain to subside making small talk about the size of the elephants. "An elephant is bigger than this tent," Jen noted in reflective astonishment. "When you see them from the truck you feel so small."

As the rain stopped we separated into our two tents. I tried to stay awake to read by the beam of my torch. I was reading *Uhuru* by Robert Ruark. I reread it every time we traveled to east Africa. Ruark's treatment of the Mau Mau unrest and turmoil of 1962 gave me a sense of place. It was hopeless. I couldn't keep my eyes open, although it was only 8:30 in the evening. It was dark. No need to stay awake.

I heard it first at a distance just beyond Jen and Ian's tent. The tent rustled and I thought Ian was making a late-night trip to the bushes. Simultaneously, I realized there was something else out there. Jen would be terrified.

I listened to a loud swishing sound which I did not recognize. I didn't move, lying on my back, my eyes open as wide as buffalo cow pies. Other sounds led me to at first believe the pigs were in camp again. It made me angry that the garbage was an open pit so close to the camp ground. My heart pounded. The sounds were heavy; I knew no pig could make such large noises. The hugeness became obvious.

I did not breathe. Whatever it was, it was very close. The sound was swishing and chewing. I worried that Daryle would turn over and rustle the noisy nylon of his sleeping bag. I worried that he would sneeze a loud midnight sneeze or cough causing 'it' to stampede.

"Dad!" Ian whisper-shouted from his tent. "Do you hear it? Do you see it? Dad, are you awake? Elephant coming right to your tent."

My heart beat like the smacks of a slap box, fast and jumpy. What if the elephant tripped on a guide wire of the tent, I envisioned the animal being startled, ripping the tent apart with one swipe of his trunk. I forgot that we slept in a pop-up dome tent with no guide wires. I forgot that elephant are sensitive enough to step around a bird nest in the dust. The chewing and chewing continued so close that I felt the rhythm of the chomps.

I dared to silently slip my arm out the top of my bag to cautiously lift the corner of the window flap. Nothing. It was black. I lifted it a bit more and looked again. The entire window frame was filled with the body of an elephant, now strolling past the back side of our tent.

I ventured a peek out the side window flap. There stood Ian in his midnight get-up standing semi-crouched next to their tent, a vision wearing safari boots, fruit-of-the-loom shorts, a desert storm floppy hat and a safari shirt; he held his bazooka camera lens with both hands.

I listened to Ian clicking the Nikon, nervous that the sound would cause alarm. If not a stampede, a stomping was still within the realm of possibility. The stride was long and quickly the pachyderm moved beyond our tent.

No one talked until morning. I venture that no one slept either, except Daryle who still falls back to sleep after waking at night. My own heart continued to pound for another hour, if not the rest of the night. Where was the wine box? I was never sure if other mammoths might follow.

They did not.

At breakfast, my midnight craving for a wine gave way to a need for caffeine. When the sleepiness subsided we all talked at once sipping steaming Kenya coffee and hot cocoa.

"That was so exciting last night," I started.

"We were lucky to see that huge elephant," Daryle cupped his tin mug.

"Weren't you scared, Dannie?" Jen asked squeezing her eyebrows together and cocking her head.

"Yeah, I was terrified. It was so exciting. I didn't breathe all night," I said, the adrenalin still pumping.

"Wouldn't it be better to get in the car or something?" Jen crossed her arms.

"I got some great photos, though it was dark. I didn't want to use a flash," Ian mentioned.

"Very wise, child," I said. Once a mother, always a mother.

"I was so scared," Jen repeated, "I reeeally needed to use the *choo*, but I didn't dare leave our tent. No way was I going outside the security of the tent."

"Yeah, like a nylon tent would protect you," Ian jibed.

"That Jen, last night, is why we love Africa so much." Daryle returned his empty mug to the table.

"You *love* that? Being scared out of your wits, endangering your lives and the lives of your family is what you *love*?" She turned toward the table as if to make herself a cup of hot cocoa.

"Wassup for today?" I changed the subject.

"We're heading for the Serengeti."

Abundance

Zebra galloped playfully as we approached the Serengeti plains; gazelle scampered over the corrugated dirt road.

From our side of the savanna we watched enormous ostrich from 500 meters across the horizon. Ostrich is the largest bird in the world with long, strong legs. We had no difficulty spotting the beauties. Jen lifted her binoculars to get a closer view.

"I wore a hat once with one of those feathers." She steadied the lenses. "Look at their legs; that's a drumstick! They seem very dainty as they step along."

I didn't mention that those dainty legs can dropkick an

opponent or rip out one's throat if provoked.

"Are those the kind of feathers they use in strip places for the *fan dance*?" She turned around addressing me.

"Well Jen, how would *I* know? And how do *you* know about strip joints?"

"Oh, well, they used to have mini scenes in the black n white cowboy films, remember? Spaghetti Westerns and really tacky low budget films, stuff like that."

"Hmm. Keep an eye out. Maybe we can find an ostrich plum along the way," I murmured.

"One year an ostrich ran in the track in front of our truck," Daryle remembered. "We clocked it at something like twenty-five miles per hour." He looked at me, "We filmed it running in front of us for ten minutes before he ran into the bushes. Remember that, Dan?"

"That was years ago, BC: Before Children." I thought of previous safaris.

Three hyena staggered along the road like disfigured, misshapen werewolves. They seemed awkward as they loped along. Their long front legs supported a furry back which sloped to meet shorter hind legs. A mane-covered, thick neck connected the body parts which altogether created a creepy creature.

Two small jackal darted across the road. I thought, it's wonderful to see so much game even outside the park.

Thousands and thousands of animals staggered across the plains: striped, furry, spotted, horned and bearded. Looking in all directions we watched as massive herds made passage across the great Serengeti plains. By comparison to drought years the animals seemed lively and healthy, running, frolicking and locking horns.

The profusion of zebra on the road made me believe again. Everywhere I turned I saw zebra. Black and white, a pattern of opposites: vertical lines 'round the bellies, horizontal stripes 'round the legs. Dark and light in conflicting harmony. For the first time I understood the term *motion dazzle*, a form of camouflage. While the bold patterns of the zebra did not blend in with the muted tones of the savanna, the abundance of contrast served to confuse the predator giving the disadvantaged zebra a better chance of escape, especially if part of a herd.

The scene reminded me of a fabric shop dizzy with design. Yet it was the living stripes that generated the power, the energy of the African migration; living, walking, trotting zebra like the old Africa with an abundance of herds and animals: uplifting and encouraging.

When the way cleared, we roared across the washboard; zebra and wildebeest galloped and cantered out of our way. The ribbed roads were a fact of African safari. What was the best strategy? Go fast and bounce incredibly, miserably along or, drive agonizingly slow over each bump of the rigid, crenelated motorway? The choices were: faster is better or slow avoids the bumps but prolongs the pain.

We sat around our campsite in Serengeti before heading out for an afternoon drive. The camp chairs served as relief from bouncing on the roads. We watched a large herd of gazelle just beyond our tents. They ran in a frenzy, hissing and coughing before darting through the trees. What were they running from? We thought we might see a kill, right at our campsite; two bucks engaged in a round of head butting then ran back and forth also hissing. They raced through the trees at breath-taking speed.

"Whoa… what's going on?" Jen was as curious as the rest of us. Then, "What's happening? What are they doing?" She lowered her binoculars.

"Think birds-and-bees, Jen."

"Oh…"

"No, I'm just kidding. Look at this. It says gazelle run up to 50 miles per hour," I handed the book to Daryle.

"Oh wow! Look! Did you see that?" Ian attempted to focus his camera.

We witnessed spectacular pronking. When the gazelle pronks, it leaps into the air, straight up like Masaai warriors leaping with both feet off the ground; the gazelle pronks with all *four* feet off the ground. The reason for this was, according to the book, perhaps for play or to alert predators.

"Wow! I wanna do that!" I jumped out of my chair and spread my arms wide. "Watch this. Pronk! Pronk! Pronk!" I leaped into the air in my best cheerleader form, arms and legs extended.

"Forget it, Mom. Okay, maybe back-in-the-day, but forget about prancing around out here in the savanna." This was truth in advertising. "You haven't really mastered the pronk. Give it up." Ian was blunt.

Even giraffe got caught up in the flow although they did not migrate. They ambled along nibbling the tops of acacia trees surveying the annual hajj from their privileged vantage; we gawked at them on both sides of the road in groups larger than usual. Still, it was the zebra that took my breath away.

For dinner, Jen and I sorted the pots and pans while the guys set up a fire pit for after the meal. We usually started with a round of gin and tonic to watch the sun go down and ease the jarring of the day; except for Jen who stuck to the tonic-only formula. The starter was a bag of salted peanuts for Jen and Ian. Daryle and I enjoyed a jar of black caviar that I brought from Saudi topped with diced Kenya onions, which dusted the Kenya crackers. Jen and Ian were not enamored with the caviar; oh well.

This night we choreographed pasta with canned tomatoes and

a can of meatballs. No fresh veggies today so we opened a can of pale, tasteless asparagus. The cheeses were pretty good. I sliced some cheddar to garnish the vegetable and tossed on a few chili flakes; Jen sliced more cheese for the noodles. Ahh, red-wine-in-a-box complemented the pasta like a best friend, like friend you've known all your life. These safaris were about animals and stories and campfires, not about gourmet camping food.

In the morning we headed toward Arusha and Mount Meru in northern Tanzania. The car started missing again. Bad gas, no gas? Cah-bah-rate-tah? Fuel line, fuel pump? What a pain. Go ahead or go back, what to do? The guys checked the tank. No leak. Should we go forward slowly? We tried to make it through a big puddle; the car died. No more engine. Hood up, they attempted to locate the problem.

I remembered a *kanga* proverb printed along the border of a bright red and orange cloth: *We are all passengers, God is the driver.* I hope the Driver gets the car moving.

Ian broke a stick off a roadside acacia, stripped its thorns and inserted the branch to determine if there was gaz. There seemed to be some. They began sucking up the petrol again. But would the big suck-up work this time? We just got petrol 30 minutes ago and now the truck was missing. The highway was good but the car was not. They fooled around under the hood, tried it again and voila, it started. Jen's prayers at work. She claims we have used up most of our nine lives. Or maybe, *God is our driver.*

There was a definite blockage somewhere, but we were on the road again.

We probably would not be able to go very far but hopefully we could get to Arusha. After a forty- five minute drive over the worst ever rock road, not pebbles but boulders, we found no campsites outside of the capital city. The afternoon sun lowered in the sky as we pressed on to Mount Meru.

We looked for something at the base of the mountain. Every muscle and bone of my body ached.

My head throbbed. Thrust and slapped against the front, side and roof of the car, my body limbs, muscles and bones felt bruised and broken. My stiff joints tense and sore, led us to nothing. No campsites.

In desperation we headed back to Arusha to look for late night hotel accommodations. We found no rooms, naught, zero, zilch. No vacancy, anywhere.

One final sign tempted us down a narrow dirt path toward "Club Africa!" We drove into a gentleman's back yard and pitched our tents for 12 US dollars. He provided a huge fire and charcoal toilet pits. What more could one want? Well shower, bed, aspirin. I felt completely wrung out.

Even the sip of scotch and the comfort of the tin cup of wine didn't help my muscles relax. Probably everyone was miserable: Daryle driving all day and Jen thoughtfully silent. We needed to eat. This was the night for MREs, meals ready to eat.

I reached into the food bin for something quick. Beef Stew. The pictures on the label like promotional propaganda promised a thick a sauce, huge boiled potato chunks, bright orange carrots, shiny round green peas and large pink hunks of prime rib. Although it was a hot meal, it tasted like hospital food, unsalted bullion with bits of surprise to provide texture: miniature diced potatoes, carrot bits, shriveled, wrinkled peas and specks of beef.

Nobody cared; we were exhausted. We sat around the fire for a while then crashed in our tents.

I did not sleep; my body ached.

This morning back in the car, we were on a blacktop road headed toward the Kenya border and Amboseli. Yesterday we all suffered with the punctured petrol tank which took three hours, the uncertainty with the constant missing of the engine, and the horrible jostling in the truck. The feeling was almost... forget it. Today would be better. A teal and black kanga in my beach basket proclaimed *Everything is all right if you love each other.*

Vintage Wine and Cotton Candy
The Last Toast

A nd it *was* better. The evening and afternoon were beautiful. Compared to yesterday, it was easy. We were glued to our Suzuki seats, held in by the seatbelts, not joy riding in a bouncy castle. Yesterday I felt like a very old woman with no business on safari. Yesterday my enthusiasm and energy left me.

Many times on this trip I thought of my mom who traveled with us in 1964, one of our first safaris. She was 42 that summer, I was 23. She and my father recently separated. She was depressed and despondent over the divorce custody settlement. The judge, in his infinite wisdom, declared that a juvenile boy, my brother, should be in the custody of his father. My mother was devastated. How could this happen? The divorce was one thing, long overdue for reasons of lack of communication and infidelity. She never anticipated losing her son. I was already out of the house, out of college, married and living in Africa, not close enough for support. At that time she felt life dealt her a raw deal. We invited her to come to Addis Ababa and join us on an African safari into Kenya and Tanganyika, as it was known. As intended, it proved the perfect diversion. She planned, read books, checked out National Geographic from the library, saved her money, got hyper excited and embarked on a fly-now-pay- later plan to arrive in Addis for a life changing trip.

Today was better. Today was good; today was fabulous; today was why we put up with the difficult life style. We decided to stay in the *bandas* at Amboseli, the home of Mount Kilimanjaro. The dust in Amboseli was fine and skin permeable. It billowed up as we safaried along. The soft red dirt wafted everywhere in the car, through the wide-open windows and narrow-closed crevices in the floorboard and doors. It adhered to our skin like Johnson's baby powder.

"This is one of our favourite places, Jen." I hauled my backpack off the floorboard.

"Cool. Why is that, Dannie?"

"Because the beautiful Mt. Kilimanjaro is hiding behind those clouds." I looked in the direction of the mountain. "The top is snow covered and the clouds keep it veiled like a protected wife." I looked back at Jen. "It's not visible very often. I hope we get to see it."

A shower never felt so welcome. The wet dust cascaded in rivulets down my arms and legs forming irrigation tracks until the slow drip of the warm shower covered the entire surface of my skin; the dust welled up in dunes at the bottom of the cement shower floor.

We enjoyed a late lunch, a corn and bean salad embellished with diced onion, vinegar and oil and fresh-ground black pepper. We gnawed slices of wild biltong. Jen made Fanta with orange concentrate and bottled water and we topped it all off with apples and peanut butter for dessert. We ate outside on the deck of our *bandas*.

The evening game drive was notable for herds of elephant. There were many young and the car seemed to pose no threat to the females with calves or the protective bulls standing guard at the front and rear. Although we crawled through the herd, stuck in a massive traffic jam there was not one raised trunk, no flapping ears, no pawing at the ground, no trumpeting. The relationship between animal and truck seemed respectful.

We noticed gnu left behind in the migration looking lonely, missing the action, plus Grants, Thompsons, ostrich, lots of swamp birds: long-legged, long necked, short billed, hooked billed, hornbill, yellow bellied, red bellied, cockatooing, feather flappers.

Heading back to the *bandas* as the sun set, the clouds began to lift from Mt. Kilimanjaro. We drove on and the top became more visible and finally the setting sun glowed pink, spun cotton candy against the snow-top mountain.

"Eyes left," I said.

"There it is," from Daryle.

"What? Ohhhh. I see it. Wow. We *are* lucky," Jen lined up her binoculars, then her camera. Ian focused his bazooka lens.

I was sure we would not see the illusive mountain top. There it was. Astounding: zebra grazing at the roadside, the mountain in the background, the classic shot; postcard quality.

In the morning after coffee, cereal sprinkled with UHT milk-in-a-box and the last can of peaches we leaped into the car to see-what-we-could-see. We meandered along.

Not far from the *bandas*, next to the road a bull elephant grazed. We stopped and turned off the engine to watch the big bull swish, swish his tail back and forth.

"Daryle, what are you doing?" Jen leaned forward. "What if he charges? How can we get out of here if the engine is off?" Her voice jacked up an octave when she was nervous.

"It's okay, Jen." Daryle tried to reassure her. "I can start up." He looked over his shoulder to the back seat, "I don't think we are a threat. He's eating."

The elephant ripped up a trunk-full of tall grass then twisted his proboscis to gently place the bouquet into his mouth. The ripping was barely discernable in the daytime, but in the quiet of night it was deafening. He stuffed the bundle of green, long grass into his already full mouth, his trunk demonstrating the flexibility of a garden hose.

It didn't fit. He held some back with the end of his snout, took a few chomps then folded-in the remainder for another mouthful. The bull stayed near the road, near the car, grazing on grass and occasionally reaching for leaves in the high branches.

We observed, I taking furious notes to preserve the moment, Jen, Ian and Daryle taking occasional photos. I often sketched when the opportunity presented but this day I made written notes at the base of the mammoth mountain.

"Jen, you bring us good luck." I poured the last of the coffee for everyone, from the thermos lodged between my ankles.

"How's that, Dannie?"

"Kilimanjaro is beginning to cloud up." I tucked the empty thermos on the floorboard. "The past two days have been the only days the mountain top was clearly visible, according to everyone around here." The snow was deep on the flat table-top. "We've been here before and never seen the top of the world." I cupped my coffee mug. "You are 'first time lucky; beginner's luck' and we all benefitted. Thanx, Girl."

"Okay, that was *easy*. I'll take credit for that!" Then, as we all heard, "I love this place. I'm already thinking how soon we can come back, right, Ian?" Jen was caught up in the moment.

"What! You workin' two jobs next year? What about the sleep-walking elephants?" Ian took a last look at the meandering pachyderm.

"I was thinking of that place we saw in the book, Treetops Lodge. That looks nice." Jen projected a sense of style and elegance.

Later in the evening at the *bandas* we enjoyed late drinks and the last of the caviar under the Milky Way with a few fireflies to twinkle in the clear sky, the African big sky. We tried to finish off the end of the food for the last supper. A tin of tuna, rice, a can of whole tomatoes for a soup, and the last of the Emmentaler cheese. It all worked, complete with the bladder of red wine which seemed to go on and on, protected, salvaged, nurtured along the way.

The border crossing back into Kenya was uneventful and we began the 80 kilometer return to Nairobi on the dusty motorway. From the road one can barely notice the Masaai *bomas* with the circular thatch-roofed huts encircled with thick dry brush to keep the lion out. The compounds were camouflaged in the bush by muted shades of earth.

This safari, the first for Jen, started with a deluge that saturated the gear. The tents were wet when we packed and with no chance to dry anything, the vehicle became a rolling sauna. Everything in the car rather than dry out, became contagiously wet.

We valued Jen's presence. She forced us to see Africa from fresh eyes, "What are they do-ing?" she quizzed. Then challenged, "You *like* that?" She absorbed and reflected thoughtfully and said little to us; perhaps she vented to Ian; perhaps she rolled her eyes. She viewed the safari from her own perspective. Nairobi was not Seattle, Spokane or Dhahran. Yes, we forced her. We kidnapped her. We loved having her along. Maybe we lived on the edge. We didn't think so. She challenged our decisions.

In the damp car the cardboard wine-in-a-box became moist and quickly deteriorated. Oh no! Protect our prize possession. When the cardboard crumbled, we nursed the aluminum-coated plastic interior, spouted bag. No one wanted the bladder to burst. We wrapped it in towels, we placed it in a plastic bowl, we cradled it between our legs on the most treacherous of roads; we hid it in the centre of the spare tire.

She made the whole trip, with even enough substance for a last toast in the hotel room after a quick shower before boarding flights back to Saudi Arabia. Would we do it again? Of course. If it was easy in Kenya or Tanzania, the mind-stretch would be minimal. If the bureaucracy seamless, the challenge less. We pursued this safari with energy as if it were the last item on our bucket list. We would be back. Jen enjoyed the dazzle of the zebra, the feathers and legs of the ostrich, the giraffe, wildebeest, flamingo and even, in the end, the midnight elephant.

Mark and Boy

When Jessica and Ian were young, six and eight, we flew to Kenya from the Philippines, rented a camper van in Nairobi and drove to Meru National Park where we met Peter Jenkins, head game warden. He gave us suggestions on where the game was that morning and where we might camp. As we talked at the ranger station, he invited us to join him and his family for lunch at the warden's residence. The generous offer seemed to mesh our personalities.

After a morning of game viewing through our pop-top camper van, we made our way to the warden's home. The ranch-style residence benefitted from a wraparound veranda with a three-hundred-sixty degree panorama of the savanna. We sat on the deck watching elephant in the distance as gazelle wandered near the house. We drank tall lemonades and the warden introduced us to his family.

"This is Siana." The warden presented his daughter. With her dusty blond hair, sparkly eyes and knobby knees she and Jessica could have been cousins. They were both eight.

"Mark will be here soon." Then to his daughter he said, "Siana, take Ian and Jessica around and show them your tree house and maybe the bikes?" As he spoke, his wife joined us. He looked toward Jessica, "Siana doesn't have many western children to play with."

"Hello, I'm Sarah. Peter tells me you work in the Philippines." She looked rather proper in a dress, like a stay at home wife and mum, a housewife; not what I anticipated. I think I expected her to be in ranger greens or dressed like a rancher with a ranch hat or riding boots maybe. We, on the other hand, wore shirts and jeans for game viewing, not safari pants sold in the shops with pockets down the pant legs and on the vests.

"Yes. We're starting our third year there."

Siana attended school in Kenya but would soon join her brother at boarding school in England. Mark was home for summer break. I couldn't imagine sending my children off to boarding school at age seven, well some days I could, but for our British friends and colleagues, early boarding school was the norm.

"Mark is eleven and a bit shy these days," Sarah told us. "He's had a rough experience." She smoothed the gathers in her skirt. "He was mauled by one of George Adamson's pet lions." She glanced at the warden

"What *happened*?" I was aghast.

George Adamson and his wife Joy were known for their work in rehabilitating orphaned lions back into the wild. They were known through a film based on her book *Born Free* where she told the story of raising a cub lion and releasing it in the wild. George and Joy Adamson catapulted to fame after the film was released.

"Well," Sarah began, "Peter drove north on a routine visit of Kora National Park where George stayed in a tented camp with his so-called *pet* lions," she raised one eyebrow. "Mark went along."

"When they arrived, George met them at the gate," she took a deep breath. "The men talked a few minutes from the open range rover, right, Peter?" Sarah looked across the room at her husband for confirmation.

Peter looked over his shoulder before continuing the story; his voice cracked as he retold the horrendous event. "I didn't get out. George and I talked from the car," he started. "George said he was fine and was expecting visitors at the end of the week, which he accepted, though feigned he much preferred avoiding the intrusions; probably even ours." I later learned their relationship was strained over various passions about saving the environment.

I listened, my mouth slightly agape, my back tense as Sarah explained: Mark sat in the front passenger seat next to his father. As the men talked, Boy, the full grown 'pet' adult lion, leaped on the bonnet of the open rover and reached through the front taking a swipe at Mark who screamed and in a state of shock kicked and sobbed in anguish as his flesh fell away. Blood gushed from his thigh as the cat scraped and mauled young Mark. He couldn't get out of the car and it took the strength of both men to wrench the lion from the boy.

"It was horrible." Sarah covered her mouth with her hand, breathed in deeply and continued. "They were a long way from medical assistance," her voice also shaky. They transferred Mark to a major city for stitches, treatment and protection from infection. He was horribly traumatized from the incident as were they; he was in private, intensive care for many weeks.

When we met Mark at lunch in Meru, he was a shy, injured young boy. He was personable and somewhat conversive.

"Your Mum told us about your accident, Mark. Are you feeling okay now?" I asked.

"Yes, Ma'am; I'm fine now, thank you."

Before sitting down to lunch he slightly winched up the cuff of his khaki shorts to show us the deep red scars on his legs and arm, the scrapes of the claws clearly visible.

From the cook-house, a rather wrinkled Kenyan helper wearing a crisp white uniform appeared on the terrace to refill the lemonade pitcher while her hefty younger colleague, also wearing white, marched out plates of mild chicken curry.

The afternoon lunch, a hot meal, was warm and satisfying, like the amber of a small fire. It was the main meal of the day and like the warmth of an emerging flame, fueled the possibility of new friendships.

During the meal the ranger told us of ten to fifteen thousand elephant deaths in the past four years due to starvation at Tsavo National Park where he worked before transferring to Meru.

Now, here in Meru National Park, he concentrated on introducing white rhino to Kenya, brought in from South Africa. He told us of his plan to utilize the Kenyan *Army*, a brilliant plan, to train park rangers to fend off the assassins of elephant and rhino; of his introduction to camel patrols to watch and secure bush areas. The murderers were heavily armed and often insurgents from Somalia. Park rangers are schooled in wildlife conservation, zoology, botany, biological sciences and veterinary skills, must know several languages and now, would be training as rebel fighters.

After lunch Sarah said, "Why don't you leave Jessica and Ian here while you go out on an afternoon game drive. It's so nice for Siana to have a 'play-date,' as I think you call it in America."

The take-away from the afternoon was that Siana and Jessica got along famously as the young hostess took Jessica and Ian around the property where they cared for young orphaned animals. As we drove to our camping spot, Jessica expounded.

"She has all these animals wandering around outside her house, Mom." To Jessica it seemed idyllic. "They were babies and something happened to their mothers." She nearly babbled. "They have dik dik things? like baby deer? but they're not orphans they just wander in and out." Jessica came up for air. "Siana gets to feed them sometimes, but she told us not to get too close to the animals because they have to release them back into the wild when they get old enough." Jessica related the information with gasps of excited energy.

"When we were sitting on the porch," Jessica prattled at rapid speed like a vervet monkey.

"Slow down," I interjected.

"Mom this huge animal jumped up. Siana said it was an awful lot," she paused. "It really scared me. She said it was a pet."

"What kind of pet was it?" I asked as she hyperventilated in the back seat.

"I told you. It was an awful lot. It looked like a huge cat, bigger than our cats, bigger than our ice chest, our igloo cooler. It scared me."

"Black spots?" I asked as I figured it out.

"I think so. Mom! It was this big." She stretched her arms wide.

"It was an ocelot." I held out the animal book. "Here's a picture of it in the game book. Was this it?" I asked.

"Well, *she* said it was an awful lot." The girls corresponded for years after Siana went to boarding school in England.

Stars, Stripes and Squares

From Meru National Park we bounced along in our rented Volkswagen pop-top camper-van north to Lewa Downs for the first of several visits. Sarah and Peter suggested we visit David and Delia Craig of Lewa Downs and camp near their property. They protected, watched over, a few rhino.

Jessica and Ian peered out the windows, hanging on as we bounced along dirt roads. Graceful impala grazed and leaped across the path as we approached.

"Look! Zebra!" Ian slid his window open to get a better view.

"Shut your window, Ian. It's too dusty," Jessica protested.

"Do you notice anything different about these zebra?" I asked. I know, I know, every vacation was a field trip. I couldn't help myself.

"What?!" Jessica asked back at me, a hint of attitude in the tone. "They have more black stripes than white?" She was much more interested in her book.

"Ha! Well, you're sort of on the right track." I twisted around to address them in the back seats. "What about you, Ian? See anything different?" The zebra trotted alongside the van then swerved away, sometimes crossing the road kicking up dust as we passed.

"Mom," Jessica clutched her Enid Blyton book, her finger marking her place, "You see one zebra, you've seen them all and I've seeeeen them all." Oh the drama. I don't know where she gets it.

"These are called Grevy Zebra." I ignored her and pressed forward with my thought, my mini info-session. "They *are* a little different because they have narrow stripes and big ears. You don't see them in very many places." I attempted to draw a reference, "The zebra we saw at Siana's place were the common zebra called plains zebra."

"Well, they're not really plain, if you ask me." Jessica pushed her hair out of her eyes; way too many hours in the van.

As we drove to the edge of the property, a simple sign posted 'Lewa Downs.' The dusty one-lane road meandered on and on slowly winding through small brush leading to the main house. No diversions, just acres and acres of low, green bush. Jessica buried herself in her book until we came to Wilderness Trails at Lewa Downs.

An hour or so after the turnoff, we pulled up in front of the main building. Daryle got out to inquire about a place to camp on the property. I opened the doors to let the progenies stretch their legs and bring renewed oxygen to their brains; the proprietors invited us in for a cupa tea while we filled out a few registration papers.

Delia and David Craig made us feel, made all guests feel, like part of the family. They brought us in; pulled us in to their reserve, their private property, their private lives. The main building where we sat was the Craig family home.

Daryle and I, Jessica and Ian sat around their table while Delia hypnotized the kids with stories of elephant walking through their gardens, knocking over trees and wires, causing havoc.

"This week, just this week," Delia pushed her cup of tea slightly. "Just this week two elephants came right through here." Jessica looked out the window where the animals passed then back at

Delia. "They ripped the tomatoes by the stock, the whole vine, and ate them. Do you like tomatoes, Jessica?"

"Well, not so much," she answered, "but my brother likes them a lot. I only like catsup." Delia gained instant rapport with Jessica and Ian. She was everyone's grandma.

"Do you see that power pole leaning over, out there in the garden?" she rested on one elbow and pointed with her other hand. "We didn't have lights for two nights. But we do have a generator." She addressed Daryle and me and also her husband, David Craig, "It's a conflict between the ranchers and the wild-life," she snitched a cookie. "The villagers have it worse than we do." She leaned in, "Their answer is to shoot and kill any animals that threaten their crops or families." Then she said, "George, can you bring more cookies, please? I think these children look very hungry," she winked at Jessica and Ian.

"We are trying to educate the villagers," David spoke with authority and kindness, "to the idea that by saving the wildlife, we can promote tourism and bring revenue to the tribes and villages." He shifted on his dining room chair. "It's a new concept, you know, that people would come to Kenya, pay money, spend money, just to see African animals." He added, "Animals that kill our villagers, forage our crops, knock down our fences."

Looking at Delia he said, "We came here in 1922 and used the land for raising cattle." He ran his fingers through his thinning hair. "That was what, Delia, fifty, fifty two years ago." His huge hand wrapped around the fragile tea cup. "We always believed there was room for everyone: cattle and wild animals."

It sounded exotic. Imagine elephant strolling through your garden. For Delia, it was problematic, not exotic. What they didn't eat, the elephants destroyed by absolute advantage of size. They knocked over telephone poles, electrical wires and ripped branches off trees of the beautiful garden.

She and David talked with grave concern of the problems of elephant poached for ivory, and rhino plundered for their valued horns. Although the game gave landowners occasional grief, the Craigs believed the animals must be preserved.

They worked closely with Sarah and Peter Jenkins, the warden at Meru National Park. Their worst fear: rhino extinction. They told us of their interest in protecting rhinos and they encouraged donations to their vision, their concept for preserving the rhino on their land at Lewa Downs. They began considering a strategic, purpose-built plan for how to save the rhino.

We drove the van to a remote area of the property which they suggested and set up camp as the group of rhino wandered close by on the other side of a sinewy wire fence. Daryle set up a small fire pit for after sunset and we set out our chairs.

I washed a few dusty t-shirts for the kids and hung them on a makeshift line to dry in the breeze while Jessica and Ian played something make believe. I loved that we never took toys on trips. They needed nothing but imagination, though Jessica did plow through books when she was somnolent from the landscape.

We set out for an afternoon drive searching for game in the area. Daryle popped up the roof for better viewing. Cool air blew through the van like a ceiling fan attached to the top of the pop-up, ventilating the minivan. Standing on the seats, Jessica and Ian enjoyed the view. They scanned the savanna like vulchers searching for a kill, popping their heads out the top.

Right away we drove through a dazzle of zebra meandering and skittering across the trail. Small families of elephant grazed and giraffe sheared the tops of acacia trees.

"You know what?" I had to point out one more thing. "These are special giraffe."

"Why, Mom"? Ian was getting into being the first to spot an animal.

"They're called reticulated giraffe." They would probably never get this, but I tried.

"Why? What does *that* mean?" Ian stood on tiptoes looking out the pop-top. "What's the difference? They look just like the other giraffe, right, Mom?"

"Stop the car, Daryle," I looked through my binoculars. "Let's watch them for a few minutes." I leaned out the window. We stopped at the side of the road as the group of giraffe nibbled away the tops of the trees. "Be real quiet so we can watch them," I whispered. "Maybe they will come closer." Daryle focused the camera.

"So why are they tickle-ated giraffe, Mom?" Ian whispered.

"It has to do with their spots." This sounded like the start of a folk tale, 'How the Giraffe Got its Spots.' "Masai giraffe," I kept my eyes on the tree tops, "the regular giraffe, have brown spots that look something like the shape of a tree leaf or a funny star," I said trying to think of how to describe the difference as I read in the guide books. "Reticulated means arranged like a net or a network, it says here." I tried again, "Sort of like a basketball net." Ian looked at me, waiting.

"They don't look like basketball spots," he whispered.

"Each brown spot is shaped like a straight-lined shape, like a math shape."

"You mean like squares and triangles," Jessica piped in.

"Something like that," I whispered back. "What shapes do you see on that closest giraffe?" I asked. "Anything you recognize?"

"Well, there's a kind-a square shape and other weird shapes." Jessica added.

"You're right," Ian figured it out. "No leaf shapes on these giraffe. I get it."

When we returned from our afternoon game drive, I noticed that the sweaters and shirts from the line were gone. Stolen. This was a profound disappointment. There were, of course local villagers working on the property. Someone needed what we had.

We were naïve to leave the items out. Enamored by our time with Delia and David Craig, we felt complete trust. Silly us. I told the kids the monkeys must have snitched their shirts. Is it okay to tell little lies to avoid difficult realities? I thought of it as 'inventing the truth.'

Although we were camping, the Craigs encouraged us to spend a night in one of their two luxury gazebos, a two room tent which rested on hardwood floors with private bath *ensuite*. They spoiled us bringing hot coffee and warm chocolate in the morning with a gentle, "Good morning, Sir."

Safari was not new to us, having cut our teeth on the safari life while working in Ethiopia. This time we took the kids to enjoy East Africa. And this time Delia and David personalized the safari.

In their kitchen-dining room we talked about their land, their project, their thoughts for the future. They supported four rhinos. They hoped to sponsor a sanctuary; a special place to protect the rhinos near where we camped.

We flew in from the Philippines, rented a van and drove to Lewa Downs.

We camped at the rhino reserve before it was a reserve with four precious rhino.

If provoked a rhino could ram the van and topple us over. We weren't that provocative.

Before leaving we bought half a rhino in support of their proposed project.

St. Elsewhere, the Milky Way and Betty Davis

When Jessica and Ian were teenagers, sixteen and fourteen, we flew to Nairobi, this time from Saudi Arabia. We rented a car and drove again to Lewa Downs. Electric wires hung from the gate. Other wires dangled low enough to tickle the heads and backs of elephant with just enough jolt to turn them in another direction. We registered, as guides hoisted the gear to our *banda*.

It felt comfortable returning to Lewa Downs, like picking up with an old friend exactly where we left off, being greeted and re-united with David and Delia Craig. Delia looked the same as she did years before when she snitched an extra cookie at tea time. She was the same loving, caring, hardworking grandma figure we knew before.

Entrenched in our *bandas*, later in the day, I sat in a camp chair behind the elegant hut. I let my hair drip-dry from an afternoon shampoo in our private outdoor shower. The sun warmed my scalp as I brushed through wet spikes of hair. My towel hung across my shoulders like an ill flung Pakistani *dupatta* while I read *Uhuru* for the seventh or eighth time.

One of the guests also staying at Lewa Downs walked past our hut. He stopped for a moment to make small talk. Mortified to be in a drip-dry state, I quietly said "Hello," barely lifting my eyes. He was equally shy, but returned the comment.

"Enjoying your book?"

"I am. You're American." I recognized the quiet accent.

He paused and looked at me with reservation. "Yes...."

"Where do you live?" I asked, knowing to never ask, "Where are you *from*?"

He looked at me again with what appeared to be suspicion. "We're from California. Where are *you* from?" he asked. He didn't know. He didn't know never to ask a Third Culture Person 'where are you *from*?' because we don't know the answer. It's a trick question. Do you want to know my nationality, my passport country? Where I grew up? Where I work, where I live now? I glossed over it.

"We live in Saudi Arabia," I said looking between wet wisps now drying without direction. "We're here with our kids," and continued, "Are you here with your son? I noticed you together last night."

"Yes," he kicked the dirt. "Just a get-away from California."

"What's your work?" I asked as I ran a brush though my hair without looking.

He looked at me again with that apprehensive look. "I work in Hollywood." He offered nothing further.

"Really. I grew up in Southern California." It was always of interest to meet someone from your home turf. "What's your work there? I'm sorry, are you in film?" I apologized; it seemed a cliché to assume that everyone from Hollywood was in film.

I couldn't read that look, but it was there again. "Well, I do some television work."

"Wonderful! Are you a writer?" I don't know why I was talking with this man. I knew

I looked like a like a wet Chihuahua in need of a blow-dry, but he was shy and kind. Then it started to sink in. I probably *should* know him.

"I'm sorry," I apologized again. "We don't get much TV in Saudi. Are you doing something important?" I can't believe I said that. "I mean, I probably should know you?" It got worse. "I apologize. What is your work?"

"I'm an actor; with a drama series."

"Oh. What's it called? Would I know it?" I sounded lame, but I had no idea.

"It's a medical drama, 'St. Elsewhere,'" he said, tilting his head while looking at me.

"I'm sorry; I don't know it."

He relaxed. He opened up.

"I brought my son who attends Hollywood High." I knew the school. "He's quite shy," he said as he pushed his hands into his front pockets, "but loves to study the stars. He'll bring his powerful telescope to the campfire tonight." He turned to leave, "See you there?"

"Sure. I think the kids have met," I ran my fingers through my now dry hair. "My kids study in boarding schools."

"Maybe, but my son is pretty quiet. See you tonight."

I still didn't know his name.

Campfire

D elia Craig, magnificent matriarch of Lewa Down, placed emphasis on homemade dinners. 'Homemade' suggested homegrown, before organic was trendy. 'Homemade' suggested recipes from her kitchen, family recipes; food that filled the soul, food that satisfied the outdoor appetite from bouncing in the bush all day. She and her staff baked hot bread every morning in a big open stone oven and prepared fresh hors d'oeuvres served each night with drinks 'round the bar.

Guests gathered for sundowners. Some craved a stiff bush

drink, a straight scotch or bourbon over ice or a neat vodka. Others clung to longer drinks. Gin and tonic was a favourite African safari drink; it stretched out the conversation and all conversation centred on the game-of-the-day: who spotted what. No one drank wine before dinner.

The backstory on gin and tonic, l learned much later, was that tonic was useful for curing malaria even preventing malaria; the quinine in tonic water was a great deterrent hence the popularity of gin with lots of tonic for the early British colonists in Africa.

We shared notes like hungry film directors; producers of some safari newsreel, a travel documentary for National Public Radio. "Where did you see the leopard?" we asked, as if it might be there tomorrow.

Delia and David Craig ushered guests into the thatch-covered dining area. "Please come in," David invited, holding the door. "Are you ready to dine? We welcome you."

The five course dinner was different each night starting with steaming soups and crunchy fresh salads; next they served a fish course followed by mains and fresh-baked desserts; all nourishing with a sense, a touch, of class; a touch of fine dining, albeit fine dining in the rough.

After dinner, after licking our forks stark naked of fresh, warm, deep dish apple pie, we moved to the campfire which burned with high intensity. Flames danced toward the stars like tiny shards of confetti. Director-style camp chairs awaited our arrival at the bonfire. The staff moved about with silver platters of liqueurs, brandies, more scotch and bourbon.

Recounting of the day's events unfolded 'round the fire where safari stories were validated through the telling, enhanced like the jawing of fishing tales. The campfire authenticated the stories. Once told at the fire circle, it must be true. If you heard it at the campfire, you were privileged to retell it as a famous safari story.

Families joined the fire circle where kids of all ages participated, listening, wide eyed and open mouthed to the narratives of game sightings and daring events of the day.

At some point, unnoticed, a young teenager assembled a tripod with an enormous telescope pointed to the firmament.

Most of us identified the Milky Way. "There it is! Oh look! The Milky Way. Look at the stars. There are gazillions of stars," everyone chimed in.

As guests took note of the articulate young man behind the tripod, they listened as he described the constellations. "There's Orion's Belt," I pointed upward. I knew that constellation and a few others. This quiet young man told about each star and cluster with knowledge and humble insight. Away from the fire pit, every star twinkled with brilliance. His father was William Daniels of St. Elsewhere fame.

Betty Davis

The Craigs offered guests an early morning horseback riding safari. "Never mind your hair, let's go," Daryle needled.

"Okay, let's go, kids," I pitched in. "Jessica, you don't need your backpack. Ian, grab a jacket."

With guides we rode amongst herds of zebra, wildebeest and giraffe. The rider became an extension of the horse, one in the same. Walking silently, surrounded by other wildlife, neither rider nor wildlife appeared apprehensive, neither appeared restless. We trekked in small groups with knowledgeable guides who pointed out details of the herds and landscape even as we nudged our horses across small streams.

From our mounts, riding in the proximity of reticulated giraffe, we gazed up and up and up their long necks to stare into enormous Betty Davis eyes.

I leaned over toward Jessica and Ian and whispered from my horse, "They have Betty Davis eyes."

"Who's Betty Davis?" from Ian.

"She was a movie star," I whispered from my horse, "with huge eyes and long eye lashes." My horse stumbled slightly and I paid attention to the reigns. "Your Nana liked her," I thought back to the films. "She made some spooky movies, but she was famous for her beautiful eyes."

Just as we started to feel a bit of tension, a touch of TB, tired buttock, we entered a small clearing where white-clothed tables set with fine silver and champagne glasses awaited our arrival. A dismount was never so welcome and the surprise elegance of the hot, steaming breakfast took our breath away.

Under the trees, buffet tables presented trays of hot sausage, bacon and slices of ham, platters of silver dollar pancakes with syrup and powdered sugar, pitchers of fresh orange juice, apple juice and stocks of bananas. Other platters offered steaming scrambled eggs with sides of hash brown potatoes and mush-rooms and onions. And for the British component, mandatory vats of hot baked beans.

We briefly greeted William Daniels and the kids said 'Hi' to the stargazer, but in the daylight, he was painfully shy and merged into the shadows after filling his plate.

One afternoon David Craig took the four of us on a walking tour of one segment of the property where they sited Stone Age tools. We thrived on locating worked pieces of flint in dried lake-beds in Saudi Arabia.

Louis and Mary Leaky, renowned anthropologists, reported findings of Early Man in Ethiopia and Kenya. On this property at Lewa Downs, David showed us scrapers and weapons left on the land. The carved and chiseled tools, made from flint of the region represented the Stone Age. All of it was on the ground, as if the residents would be back in the afternoon to gather their implements.

These pieces were exact replicas of the items we discovered on camping weekends out of Riyadh, as if the lands merged at one time and nomads from the Paleolithic or Neolithic period roamed, migrated with the herds.

David pointed out the flint with a walking stick or a point of his dusty shoe, all of it left on the ground as if just discovered that day. David Craig removed nothing. Left it for the inquiring traveling soul. He did have a mini museum of artifacts, with a few notes from Louis and Mary Leakey. But David made it quite clear that the examples were to remain in the dirt. I was inclined to lift them, slide one or two in my pocket. I respected his thinking.

In 1974 we camped at the rhino reserve before it was a reserve with four precious rhino. We flew in from the Philippines, rented a camper van and drove to Lewa Downs. Eight years later, 1982, we flew in from Saudi, rented a car and stayed in a posh tent and always, always supported the rhino sanctuary. The Craigs determined that refined, high end camping enabled profits. Wealthy tourists wanted to share the land and animals and proved willing to support the project in exchange for luxury. They, and a major funder, made generous donations for what was to become the Lewa Wildlife Conservancy.

After their retirement to Malindi on the Kenya coast in 1991, Peter and Sarah Jenkins assisted David and Delia Craig of Lewa Downs to set up the first private wildlife conservancy in Kenya.

We always believed the rhinos were 'our rhinos.'

Camping With the Masaai

Suzanna met us at the entrance of the *enkang* with a large child affixed to her hip. They were as two pieces of Velcro; his long legs dangled at her side like the long legs of a locust. We almost missed the *enkang* passing it in a billow of dust. The compound fence, made of dried shrubs, tumbleweed and thorn bushes, blended with the flavorless colour of the earth as it enclosed the Masaai compound.

Villagers made the barricade by weaving a few twigs parallel to the ground, through upright dead branches, sticks and trees, tightly woven to keep out predators: cats, hyena and jackal. It also served to keep the goats and cattle in, and to keep vegetarians out of the maize crops.

"Tati," Susanna said referring to her husband, "will come soon." She adjusted the load on her hip.

Daryle drove the car across the road and I walked over to help set up our tent in this Masaai village. The winds gusted on the plateau a hundred meters from Tati's garden *shamba*.

We labored for forty-five minutes to get our simple pop-up tent assembled. A small group of kids and young adults gathered to watch us struggle with the tent. Daryle and I tried to put up the rain fly but the stress was too great and the poles began to split. We gave up. We double-staked the tent floor to the ground and moved the truck to act as a wind block, but it made little difference. Several hours later, as the wind subsided somewhat, we tried again with the rain fly. We affixed it over the tent, lashed it to the car with bungees and it still flapped furiously in the wind.

When Tati returned, we were introduced.

"*Jambo*, Tati," Daryle extended his hand. "We have heard much about you from Mr. Gary."

"Welcome, *Karibu*," he said, standing thin and tall in khaki pants and t-shirt. "Thank you for coming, *asanti sana*." Tati stretched his arm toward the huts. "Please, *tafadali*," and gestured for us to come into his *enkang* where there were several huts.

Traditionally, women made the houses and Suzanna made their home of wet cow dung and straw, plastered over a circular woven stick frame. The doorway was low and narrow. The door might be of hide or perhaps wood, or perhaps there was none at all. The house was about twenty-five square meters. The openings were four to six inches wide, three inches high allowing for ventilation, if not a view.

"A woman is not chosen because of her ability to make a mud hut," Tati leaned on his walking stick polished smooth from years of use. I was glad to hear that. "She is expected to learn this from her mother," he ran his hand over his close-cropped scalp. "A girl must watch her mother at all times to learn cooking, making of the hut, caring for the cattle, caring for the children, siblings, gardening and tending the cook-fire," he measured us like a compassionate college professor. "All women know these things." He concluded, "And of the animals, all children learn."

As he spoke I thought, women seemed equal to men. On reflection I thought, women carry out the bulk, make that *all*, of the work. I learned the meaning of this social structure years later from a Masaai named Duma, Cheetah, at Ol Pejeta.

"Please, Mama," Tati addressed me directly. It felt awkward coming out of Saudi Arabia where men do not address women, nor look them in the eye. "Would you like to see our home?"

"*Asante sana*," I answered in familiar Swahili.

I bent over to enter through the low, narrow doorway. I felt blinded by the darkness and saw nothing. Going into the blackness felt like entering a dark tunnel. I sensed a narrow corridor. Tati took my arm and said, "We keep goats here, in this first room." The chamber seemed small in the dark.

"Sit here," he said still holding my wrist in the ebony stillness. Suzanna prepared a maize gruel over smoky branches and coal. Low stools on the dirt floor surrounded the small cook-fire. "You like to take photo?" Tati asked, a sensitive issue with Masaai and particularly thoughtful of him to offer. In the darkness of the small hut there was no way I could focus. I aimed and hoped for the best.

Suzanna squatted over the hot, smoky fire. She fanned it to keep it lit as billows of smoke choked the small hut. Behind her and slightly elevated was a sleeping platform covered with hide.

"Susanna and the children sleep here," Tati said. "I sleep on this side." I could now see his extended arm indicating the other side of the cooking area.

Suzanna wore superb earrings, long beaded spirals.

"Oh, Susanna," it sounded like the start of an American folk tune. "I like your earrings."

"I like your earrings, too," she replied and reached across the fire. Her fingers touched my large brass hoops and my little lizard ear-climber.

Gary later told us their oldest girl died two years earlier. Tati was very depressed for many months and came from the *enkang* to Nairobi often. Gary knew no other details.

Residents came up to welcome us with a handshake and greeting of 'soupa.' All of the women, each with a child perched on her hip or tied to her back, and all of the men shook our hands and made us feel welcome. It stunned me that these Masaai men and women wanted to acknowledge my presence, so unlike our eleven years in Saudi. Even the Bedouin families of the desert stayed separated in the tents though the Bedouin women did drive the pickup trucks to help with the goats.

"I like your scarecrow," I complimented Tati. The figure, draped in red plaid Masaai cloth, was essential to keep out the crows and huge black kites. Not unlike the Saudi scarecrows who wore long, white *thobes* and red checkered *ghutras*,

"Does it work?" I asked Suzanna.

"I think it helps, Mama," she raised the back of her hand to her mouth to hide her giggles. In Tati's garden *shamba* he grew sweet corn and long green beans.

As we walked to the cars across the road toward our tents other Masaai men greeted us with "Mama! Soupa! Sir! Soupa! " They expected to shake my hand. Eyes averted to the ground, I did not acknowledge. Then I realized they anticipated my response and expected me to be included, as Masaai women are part of the total family and social environment. I was still embedded in Saudi culture.

We sat in the cold air; the men gathered wood for a fire, I made notes on my computer. Tati came up to see what I was doing. I showed him the liquid words. Not knowing if he could read, I typed:

J...a...m...b...o, saying the letters slowly as I typed. Then I read, '*Jambo!*' he laughed; the others laughed with excitement. Then I typed, without reading the letters: T...a...t...i. He looked at the screen for a moment, then read "Tati!" more glee and laughter.

The next person was E...r...e...e...r, the *askari* who accompanied Gary and his son Chris. He spelled his name and I typed. More glee! Two others spelled their names in English or pronounced them so that I could type phonetically.

All four were given the chance to type their own names. Looking at the screen they tried to locate the letters on the keyboard; Tati hesitantly poked the T. He was surprised at how easily the key went down and excited to see his own T reproduced on the screen. Then the A, which he held down too long, causing it to repeat AAAAA. I corrected and he completed typing his name. He was proud to know how. I was proud of him too.

We sat in the cold air around the warm fire; we *mzungu* rested in camp chairs, the Masaai squatted in the dirt. Their thick toes protruded through black tire sandals, toenails uneven, unkempt. Long legs, striated muscles outstretched, reached toward the fire.

Villagers from the region seemed drawn to the fire like game to a waterhole. The men wrapped red-plaid wool blankets, not unlike Polynesian sarongs, around their tall, lean bodies. Additional blankets hugged their shoulders and shrouded their heads reminiscent of Christian Madonnas. Some gripped walking sticks, polished from continual use. Several stood tall, balanced on one leg, the other leg rested its foot on the opposite knee. The sticks, I read, were to replace spears which the government now forbids. When I mentioned this, none of the men knew of the communique and later showed up with spears.

Philip, the school master, joined us at the fire.

"Where is your school, Philip?" Daryle felt, if not a bond, an interest.

"It's very near, Sir," Philip hugged his knees as he sat in the dirt. "Only forty-five minute walk from here."

"Who attends your school?" Daryle nodded and pulled on his pipe.

"I have about 200 students," he said looking into the fire. Philip wore khaki pants and a loose shirt. "Most are boys. One-hundred-ninety-five are boys." He said 195 were boys, but I think something was lost in the translation; I'm not sure he understood the question.

"Often, only one child from the selected family," he added, "is allowed to attend school." He poked a stick in the coals.

"Does it cost a lot of money?" I asked.

"It is not necessarily the first born, or the boy," he skirted the question, "but the one who will not watch the cattle."

"Oh!" I laughed out loud.

"The responsibilities are shared and someone must always tend the goats and cattle."

Philip told us he grew up in the area near Tati's *enkang* and went to school there as a young boy. He went to one of the local colleges for two years to become a teacher, then came back to his former primary school and taught for two years, moved to another area to teach for several years and was now the headmaster in charge of the school.

"My wife is not learn-ed" he said, "but I try to teach her to read and write *Maa*." I wondered how they met. "I don't have much time because now I'm home only on the weekends and she must also tend our few cattle."

"Does your wife travel to Nairobi with you when you go?" Who wouldn't like to get to the city, I supposed.

"Oh no," he said. "She must stay with the baby and the cows and goats." He continued, "Of course, if she wanted to go to Nairobi," he stroked his chin, "just for a visit," then poked the coals again, "I could arrange that for her."

"I guess the cows are a big help to your family," I edged my chair closer to the fire and rubbed my hands together. "You must do well," I hoped I didn't sound invasive, "as a teacher and with cattle." He seemed so candid. "You have some salary from teaching, and some security from the cows."

"Oh no. I just have a few cows."

The conversation turned to "Moses" whom we did not know and who was not present.

"The problem with Moses," someone said, "is that he is well educated and speaks good English but he drinks too much." This conversation was in English and I wasn't sure if it was for our benefit or if these community issues came up naturally at any communal gathering.

"And everyone knows he snorts snuff," from someone on the other side of the fire.

"What do you drink?" Daryle asked the group.

"Honey wine. We make".

"Where does Moses get snuff?" Daryle asked. "Is it legal?"

"He gets it from a man's wife who makes it," someone answered.

The man sitting at the fire next to me, with the scraggly toenails and thick toes imbedded in his tire sandals, opened a horizontal tube which he wore around his neck. He gave us something, perhaps mistakenly thinking we would like to snort.

It looked like dirt. We analyzed it. Daryle tasted it.

"It tastes like it has sodium or salt." They tried to translate what it was. Finally they decided it was tobacco. Daryle pulled out his pouch and took out a pinch. He held out his palm and 'round the fire circle they each smelled it.

"Ah, yes."

"This is it."

"This is very strong. Very good."

Daryle gave them what little was left of his Captain Black. It *was* strong, not meant to be snuffed or snorted. *"Asanti sana,"* echoed round the circle.

Around the warm fire, Tati sneezed into his hands and rubbed the mucus between his palms like a lubricant. Disgusting? Perhaps not, as the Chinese find it disgusting to blow mucus into a cloth to be saved and placed into ones pocket.

The wind blew. The air at eight-thousand feet was cold.

✶ ✶ ✶

The tent held; the wind gusted, the tarp flapped, but the tent held. In the morning we dismantled our camp and headed out with Tati as our guide.

Dodging craters is full time and requires two-handed dedication to the wheel. Whatever side of the road you are driving, there are always less holes on the other side. The driver constantly dodges the craters, the goats, the cattle, the kids, back and forth across oncoming traffic.

It is impossible to describe the roads by photo, although we tried, or by verbally painted description: crevices, ruts, washboard, black cotton, red clay, gravel, boulders or grass. This pitted tarmac patch, potholed and eaten away at the shoulders like an irregular coastline, seemed like a highway-marvel by comparison to other dusty trails.

We escaped a broad-side collision with an oncoming car which swerved in soft sand to avoid a pothole. The driver lost command of the car. As he passed, he came at us veering and fighting for control. We speeded ahead, avoiding the tragedy. Add to the mix bonus points for missing the cattle, goats and the children who guide them. Driving in Africa is a cross between a Chinese fire-drill, Russian roulette and American dodge ball.

* * *

Every ten years or so a new generation, a new age-group of boys, transition from childhood to young warriors, circumcision the apex of the event. The young men live together in a *manyatta* near their family *enkang* for several years to learn hunting and survival skills.

The days we visited with Tati, we were privileged to observe some of the celebrations for this ceremony as the adolescent boys became initiated into the next age-group, their transition to *morani*, warriors. The warriors, as a group, later become junior elders, then full elders, always as an age-group.

We stopped at one village, though all communities in the area prepared for this occasional age-group event. Daryle, Gary and Chris wandered off. I sat in the dirt, leaning against a hut making notes on my computer.

The circumcised boys, dressed in black, wore splendid feather head pieces. They stood in groups of threes and fours looking over my shoulder at my computer screen. They leaned against the hut and against their walking sticks, sometimes standing on one leg, the other bent, the foot resting on the opposite knee. I could not look backward at them and type at the same time, consequently I tried to distract them with the movement of my fingers while I concentrated on how their halos were constructed.

Someone explained that as the boys shot a bird, the bright feathers went onto the headpiece each representing a different species; the more the better, and the more colourful. Ostrich feathers made up the largest crowns.

A flock of young children sat on the ground around me, even sitting on my feet. Preoccupied with my brown leather shoes, they touched them; they stroked the suede and the rubber soles. They imitated the motion of my fingers on the computer, as I used to play the piano on the desk top when listening to an orchestral piece.

A shy three-year old wanted to be part of the group. When our eyes met, she ran away. Her chubby cheeks glowed with sunshine and health and she was bedecked with a necklace, and bracelets around her plump wrists.

After running away many times, she came in close to me. She bore a white V painted on her forehead between her eyes. She sported beads around her tiny ankles, still thick with baby fat. The hem of her navy wrap-around was even beaded at her knees. A final fabric tied around her shoulders under her beads, completed her ensemble. The cherub wore several small keys on a multicoloured beaded necklace.

I watched as several women approached a *banda*. They slaughtered a cow for the celebration and hauled the slab of red meat inside. Carried in outstretched arms, the bloodied head of the cow, hacked off by a *panga*, was unceremoniously taken into the dark hut.

Someone else carried other parts. Inside they cleaned a goat. Its full body laid outstretched and skinless near the door opening. They removed the stomach. A woman took the bladder, or large stomach, outside the hut and emptied green liquid from the sack, sliding her thumb and forefinger the length of the pouch forcing and squeezing the bile-green innards from the pouch-container-gut. A pet dog trotted up licking the innards. The woman prodded it away with her bare foot.

We were invited to another dark hut. I noticed the woman of the *banda*. She wore earrings. Enormous earrings: three inches wide and very long. I felt an immediate connection with this woman who stood tall in front of her home, one hand on her hip; with her other hand she scrubbed her teeth with a short stick.

Beaded strips of leather looped through her stretched earlobes. I stared in astonishment. Attached to the base of each leather strip, a strand of glass beads dangled down another four inches. The thread of beads gave the appearance, the illusion, of a necklace though it did not reach behind her neck but hung, draped from each earring, to the center of her chest. I envisioned this bush elegance at the theatre, the opera, the office.

I admired the ensemble; I went crazy-going-out-of-my-mind from the beauty of this creative piece of adornment, in the middle of the Masaai bush. As I marveled, she took them off and hooked the leather into my own huge, generic, brass loops, my own lobes having only a small pierced hole. The earrings were heavy but dramatic. I wanted that piece of art; I coveted those beautiful ear pieces; but I could not take them from her. Oh how I wanted, hoped, fantasized to see them in the gift shop of an African Hotel or Nairobi Museum Shop. I knew they would not be found in a shop. They were unique, made in her village or traded from a nearby village.

I wanted a picture of this woman, this art aficionado. I wanted my picture with her. I knew it was not allowed during the ceremonial time. This striking soul led us inside her shadowy hut. I saw nothing. There was a small window hole but someone sat in front of it and no light came in. I groped my way to the side of the fire. The structure of the hut was similar to Tati's house. This, however, was the hut, the home, of the African Earring Goddess.

* * *

I sat on the hide which acted as the bed platform slightly elevated from the fire. There was another sleeping area across the small room on the opposite side of the fire. In each room I noticed aluminium trunks with pad-locks. What treasurers would be locked in these mud huts? It must be where she kept her earrings.

"How large is your family?" I asked the Goddess.

"I have three children," she said, then rubbed her stomach in a circular motion. "One more coming," I noticed the slight swelling under her *kanga*. I looked around the hut.

One trunk at the front of the room was open, packed with pieces of *kanga*-type cloth and a mirror. My eyes adjusted to the dark and I watched as she unlocked a container in the adjacent room, now…. to show me her collection of Masaai jewelry. I shifted my weight in anticipation.

She inserted a small key, and as I held my breath, the Goddess slowly turned the lock. She lifted the tin lid as I leaned in to glimpse at the contents. Inside: cooking utensils. This woman was utilitarian as well as artistic. She removed two tin cups.

Young toddlers wore keys on beaded strands around their

necks. We often saw them, bare-naked alongside the road as they leaned on a little stick in charge of the cattle and goats, maintaining the family wealth. Chewing a piece of grass or a twig, the boys wore nothing but the inevitable beads, or copper, twisted around wrists and ankles, perhaps a cloth around them which blew in the breeze exposing all. With a *kanga* tied over their shoulders or under their chin as a cape, flowing, billowing over a tucked-in knee-length sarong, girls like the boys, tended the animals.

Children stretched their earlobes from a young age. As they played and herded cattle, twigs and sticks stuck, wedged, through their pierced holes. As the lobes stretched, some might insert empty tin cans to further extend their droopy ears. It reminded me of stories read to me as a child, of islanders who stretched their lips by inserting disks, then plates, as I recalled those vividly illustrated stories.

As professionals, adult Masaai men often in place of earrings, looped their lobes over the top of their ears, as if the extended, elongated sections got in the way.

Space, Flies and Primping

B ack outside, we shuffled along a narrow, dusty footpath to another compound. Daryle and I, Gary and Chris followed Tati and others from the *enkang*.

"*Sopa! Sopa!*" we called out. Invited inside the small opening of the dried thorny fence, residents introduced us to the chief who sat in front of his hut on a straight-back chair. He was perhaps seventy, his skin leathered and wise from bush life. He wore thick glasses in old, black, plastic frames, long ago broken and held together with a piece of tape wound around the bridge holding the right lens to the left like twins holding hands.

We were invited inside a hut but it was dark and already crowded, claustrophobic to my western culture. I needed the "outline of *space*, to be distanced by a protective spatial aura," I read somewhere, perhaps from Nadine Gordimer. I declined the invitation.

"Hmm," I breathed scanning the compound. The operative word-of-the-day: flies. Flies covered the babies. "There's dung everywhere," I whispered to Daryle as if he didn't notice. The child's arm could not be distinguished from the blanket of flies. "You just have to walk through it," I said from the side of my mouth, "like everyone else." At least I wore shoes.

Flies stuck to the corners of their mouths like grease stains on a shirt. The black blemishes walked along their lips, lined the insides of their broad nostrils. They settled in the corners of their eyes, yet the children did not flinch. They did not raise a hand or wrist to dislocate the menacing carriers of disease. If they smeared the mucous stream beneath their noses, they enabled more territory for the black-green creatures with translucent wings. Yet the children seemed healthy, fat and happy.

The women repaired huts with the muddy dung while youngsters ran and played, their bare toes in the soft excrement. Mud, flies and children; the cycle continued. I read that Masaai considered flies as departed ancestors, hence permitted them to linger in their eyes, nose and sores.

Young men, soon-to-be warriors, stood close together, shoulders touching, facing each other in a tight circular group. The new fighters danced in ceremonial rhythm. They jumped together, a flat-footed jump, synchronized, bounding off the calloused balls of their feet, sometimes propelling the circle forward, sometimes remaining in one place.

"Look at the little ones," I nudged Daryle. "They're pretty good," I squinted and shielded my eyes from the sun. "They must be four or five," I guessed, watching a group of boys. From an early age they practiced jumping. We watched them project their tiny bodies into the air, pushing-off from the ground, often with a lopsided thrust from a favoured leg, heels kicking their tight little bare muscular buttocks.

At another hut the men offered us honey wine. It was a mild *tej*. I gritted my teeth to sieve out the living and dead floating and swimming elements and swallow the cloudy, yellow brew. It was mild and quite good. I made a coughing gesture as if it was strong; not sure if women were supposed to drink. I pretended it was a macho beverage, to be safe. The men laughed and the women giggled and raised their hands to cover their mouths. We asked if the warriors would dance. Gary asked if they would dance for the Mama. That's me. But they were not ready and shy.

Off to another compound with Tati in the lead. This time there was no thorn fence. This was a *manyatta* built especially for the young, new warriors. Warriors don't need fences, warriors are awesome; warriors are well, warriors. This also was temporary housing to be burned down after the ceremony. The elders greeted us with '*sopa*' and handshakes and we were again graciously invited into the compound. The children gathered as if we were the ice cream truck stopping by.

The strong, young warriors outlined their faces with red paste, ochre makeup, with a distinct line sculpting the perimeter of their faces, leaving a circle of natural dark brown around their features accentuating their eyes, nose and mouth. These men knew the definition of handsome. The makeup enhanced their plaited braids, woven close to their scalps and caked with red-orange ochre.

Their hair, parted across the top, from ear to ear, divided the coiffure. Over their foreheads, the men wore tiny braided strands like long bangs pinched together with an ornament. Other braids hung down their brown backs. All would be shaved off by their mothers at the end of the ceremony.

Each warrior carried a spear like a toddler drags around a blanket. When they entered a hut they thrust the javelins into the earth outside the door, as the Japanese leave their shoes, or the cowboys check their guns; as college boys leave a necktie when involved at a dorm room.

Young girls looked impressive and coquettish for the young warriors. The girls were proud of them, as were the families. The men strutted with confidence. They looked good. They felt good.

The new warriors started to dance. They plunged their spears into the ground to the side of the group. Together, they bent their knees and lowered their shoulders in rhythm. Mudded-up with red clay from head to toe, their hair glistened.

A group of junior warriors inducted at a previous ceremony stood behind, heads shaved, in contrast, singing and incanting with the new inductees. One at a time, or perhaps two dancers, entered the centre and jumped to the dance. They lifted off the ground, pushing from their ankles a meter off the ground. Effortlessly, the balls of their thick soles thrusting, projected them upward. The melodious songs, chant-like, seemed enhanced by shoulder motions and by throwing their necks back even as they jumped.

The girls of the same age-group, sang at the outer edge of the circle which continued to expand as additional warriors joined the group. The girls wore many beads and many styles of necklaces, bracelets and anklets but of special note were the shoulder-wide neck harnesses which they bounced by lifting their shoulders in time to the songs. They were not accompanied by drums or instruments of any type but the girls knew exactly when to stop the mesmerizing movement of their neck pieces, even though the words of the songs went on.

We drove to one last compound where the young men were about to graduate from their training to become full warriors. They would not hunt lion as a ritual, but were now qualified to protect their *enkangs* and *manyattas* and their precious cattle.

As we drove up, young men dressed in full ceremonial dress including ochre plaited braids, earrings and beads, burst toward the car in an eruption of enthusiasm, not overly gregarious though typical teenagers. They crowded around the car to primp in the windows and side mirrors. They checked their hair and jewelry and red ochre makeup. They practiced jumping and lifting their shoulders in ritualistic dance beat. Everyone from the *manyatta* came to shake our hands and '*sopa*' us.

Inside, the older men sat on logs, drank honey wine and sang. These were the fathers and friends of the boys who completed circumcision. They were proud. One incanted, the others chanted ahuuummm.... ahuuummm, a deep tune accentuated by stretching and extending the neck. The elders entered in with perfect harmony as if scored by a London musician. It seemed similar to a blessing for the boys.

This age-group of girls, dressed exquisitely for the ceremony, primped without ceasing for the new warriors. They also captured their reflections in our car windows and fidgeted with their jewelry in the side-view mirrors.

Their headbands and head pieces resembled tiaras with rigid strands of beads jutting upright and to the sides like a fireworks display with beaded wires and arrows and triangles of aluminium sparkling as they dangled. They wore necklaces which reached the width of their shoulders, anklets by the dozens and bracelets by the kilos. Earrings reached down their necks dusting their shoulders, swaying as they walked. These young fashionistas pierced their ears on the upper rim as well, sometimes causing the tops to fold over by the weight of the higher ear bangles.

Riveted, I watched these girls, their manners so teenage, their dress so Masaai.

Adagio for Strings

He sat slumped in a large overstuffed chair. Samuel Barber's *Adagio for Strings* played on the stereo. Solemn, somber, sober. It was the funeral and we were not there.

We should have attended. We hesitated not wanting to infringe on personal family grief. We grieved alone in Nairobi, in the dark, dank home of a colleague who was away for the summer. The *Adagio* confirmed the mood.

The week before, we enjoyed drinks and hors d'oeuvres with colleagues and new friends. Connie Bufford collected an eclectic group for a dinner party including the manager of Bata Shoes Kenya, a couple of golfers and Mike Eldon, an IT computer administrator. We arrived from Saudi to use Connie's place in Nairobi for a summer base as we headed out on safaris.

Along with martinis we consumed samosas stuffed with spicy potatoes, chilies and cumin, and spring rolls filled with pork and glass noodles, then gathered around the long dining table of the old Nairobi colonial home.

Connie maintained a drawer of tapes of all genres including jazz, classical, pop and opera and also a stack of vintage vinyl records. As we moved from the living area with our drinks to the dining room, she changed the jazz to classical for dinner.

During the soup course we discussed the problems of the world like news analysts but void of political bias. In some ways we understood the issues with a sensitivity that outsiders didn't comprehend. We discussed topics, stabbing at wise resolutions from our Western perspective. We talked about King Fahd of Saudi Arabia and Daniel Arap Moi in Kenya from a conversational perspective rather than a profound, intimate point of view, which none of us really possessed; it was a dinner party.

The discussion swelled like a bush fire on the savanna from politics to kids, back to politics; always back to kids. Our own offspring worked in Saudi Arabia in education, Mike's son was in Somalia as a freelance photographer for Reuters, Connie's son was headed back to the States for university. As often comes up in these conversations, we wondered, "Have we done the right thing dragging our children around the world?" None of us had the answers, only the questions. Our kids were worldly, not street-smart.

Connie talked about her teenagers, Warren a recent graduate of International School Kenya and Mary still in school. Mary, a creative, inventive adolescent, whose room we occupied in her absence, exhibited vibrancy in the imaginative, artistic, mosaic museum of her bedroom walls. Warren, more inhibited and subdued occupied a barren room exposing none of his personal emotion. Perhaps he packed his life off to college.

"Dan's a free spirit," Mike said of his son. "Not yet interested in college." He looked around the table. "Says he needs time," he lifted one eyebrow, cocked his head and scooped a forkful of rice, "whatever that means." He fingered the base of his wine glass, unconsciously encircling the droplets of condensation. "Wants to go where he feels needed," he said looking at Connie. "He's twenty-two, a known photo journalist," he shrugged his shoulders. "I guess he's doing what he wants and what he does well."

"Dan's always been creative with all kinds of art, with collage and with his camera," Connie crooned in her slow, southern drawl. She leaned on her elbows and looked around the table, her chin resting on her knuckles. "You know he was respected by everyone his senior year at ISK," the International School, Kenya, she said to the group. "How long will he be in Somalia?" The question lingered, hung heavy in the air.

"Dan travels with his camera," Mike cut the tender curried meat. "He's producing postcards and T-shirts to publicize the horrible, desperate conditions in Somalia," not answering the question. "His work is rather good," he dabbed at his mouth with his linen serviette. "Hey! Okay, I'm his dad," the grin on his face broadened, "but he has a market for his sensitive photo postcards and articles." He took a swallow of wine. "*Newsweek* and *Time Magazine* printed double page spreads of some of his photos this week."

"I'd love to see his work," I said. "Where can I get it?" I leaned forward to make my point.

"I'll send the driver with a packet tomorrow." The kitchen staff came around with platters of chicken curry and rice. "Dan's returning to Nairobi next week," he looked at the host. "I'll be really glad to see him." He helped himself to more curry. "This is great food Connie, congrats to your cook," he nodded to the chef, hovering at the kitchen door. "I know Dan feels the stress and tension in Mogadishu. Said he's fed up. He's ready to get out; ready to come home." I recognized his anticipatory sense of relief at his son's homecoming. "His mum is very worried. Dan told me last week he's looking forward to a break, can't wait to get out of the tension."

The phone rang and the cook said the call was for Doctor Russell. "You can use the phone in the den; it's private," Connie indicated. I stiffened, wondering who would call us in Nairobi. In a few minutes Daryle handed me the phone and returned to the table.

"It's Ian, Connie." Daryle pulled out his chair. "He's changing his graduate program and just wanted to check in. He says 'hello.'"

When I returned to the table, there was a slight pause in the conversation. I jumped in. "Speaking of kids, here's a story about Ian and Jen," not sure why I felt compelled to share this tale about our kids. The whole evening seemed to focus on our collective expatriate families and adult offspring.

"Ian's wife, Jen, made her first trip to Africa at spring break this year. Everything was a huge eye-opener. Every-thing," I said slicing through a moist piece of chicken. "They work in Saudi," I added a scoop of rice.

"We drove to the rim of Ngorongoro Crater, set up our tents then drove down into the pit of the depression." The staff refilled the wine glasses "Of course it was fab-u-lous," I exaggerated for dramatic effect. "The rhinos were prehistoric with double horns."

"Was she scared or was she excited?" asked the man from Bata Shoes.

"Jen was amazed." Then I simulated Jen's voice in falsetto, "I can't wait to write my parents." I continued in my own voice, "We saw several lion prides, a few elephant and zebra, and astonish-ing African bird life," I said then babbled on, "You know how it is? Driving up, out of that deep crater with the switchbacks? It's so steep," I munched on a chapatti, "you have to take it in four-wheel drive." I looked around for confirmation.

"Will you get on with the story?" Daryle knew I was prone to embellish.

"Okay, okay," I said.

"I woke in the wee hours to hear something in the distance just beyond Jen and Ian's tent," I paused for effect. "Then the tent rustled," I waved my fork around to make a point. "I thought Jen was climbing out of the thing to make a midnight pit stop," I sipped at my ice water. "Simultaneously, I realized Jen would *never*," I jabbed the air for emphasis, "be outside her tent. There was something else out there."

"Dad!" Ian said through a muffled murmur. "Dad. Do you hear it?" He whisper-shouted.

"Whatever it was, I knew it was huge. At first I thought it

might be a hippo, but that didn't make sense." My table mates waited knowingly, for the revelation. "A rhino, if alarmed, would kill us, right?" I looked at the tennis shoe rep.

"I lifted a corner of the tent window flap." I made my eyes open wide. "Nothing. Completely black." Connie, not known to be a camper, leaned on her elbow, her jaw dropping as I spoke. "I couldn't even see the stars. I looked again." I milked the suspense like the best of story-tellers, like a female Ernest Hemmingway.

"The belly of a massive elephant enveloped the entire tent window. Of course it was all black." I paused in my narration, leaned back and sipped another swallow of water, then leaned in and continued. "No one breathed except the beast that inhaled slowly, then exhaled, sounding like the expiring air of a spent accordion. It not only breathed, but chomped on the grass. The molars ground in a slow rhythm as it padded along next to the tents.

"Jen was terrified and exhilarated in the morning," I chased the last bits of basmati rice around my plate. "We all were."

"So that's it?" Daryle ragged on my story.

"Well, it was pretty exciting, and for her first trip to Africa, it was a major event." Others chimed in with stories about their kids and living as global nomads as they all were, third culture kids.

In the morning, as promised, a brown envelope with photo postcards and articles by Dan Eldon arrived just before we took off for a week of camping. I skimmed the provocative photos and cards. Dan Eldon presented photo portraits, postcard art, of Somali kids laughing, smiling, playing in poverty and in war. The car loaded, we headed for safari on the African plains.

On the third night out we enjoyed sundowners and listened to the BBC news on our shortwave. While munching peanuts we learned of riots in Mogadishu and of four reporters stoned in the streets during a demonstration. We both paused. The broadcast listed no names, perhaps pending notification of kin. We ate our dinner in silence, each with our own thoughts. Over fireside drinks we wondered aloud and dialed for additional news details. None were forthcoming.

When we returned to Nairobi several days later we read the devastating headlines that Dan Eldon was stoned and beaten to death in Mogadishu days before his scheduled return to Kenya. The memorial would be the following day at the beautiful Ngong Hills.

It was the funeral for Dan Eldon and we were not there. We should have attended. Daryle sat slumped in the large overstuffed chair. Samuel Barber's *Adagio for Strings,* Connie's vinyl record, played over and over, solemn and somber. We hesitated not wanting to infringe on personal family grief. We grieved alone in Nairobi, in the dark, dank home of our colleague who was by then away for the summer.

Osh

There was no cliff to rush the beast toward, only the open meadow. Osh felt his breathing quicken. His bare feet scarcely touched the grassy earth. He clutched his blade. Others threw spears and stones.

Osh hesitated to release the blade; the blade he carved with Grandfather's guidance, the blade that symbolized everything between the young man and his mentor grandfather.

As the wildebeest rushed toward the side of the circle in a desperate attempt to escape, it ran directly toward Osh. Energized by the thrill of the hunt, Osh ran forward toward the wildebeest, with all of the power of his strong legs. He gripped the blade firmly and rather than throw it in an attempt to slow the crazed animal, in the instant it brushed his body, he thrust the blade into the neck. Man and beast fell to the ground.

The clan gathered around and continued to stone the creature quickly ending its life. The rush of the kill made way for vibrant, jubilant jumping and chanting as the hunters celebrated obtaining food for their families. When wind returned to his exhausted body and his lungs filled with air, Osh slowly joined in the celebrations. Grandfather shuffled forward to embrace Osh.

***

To Grandfather's thinking, Osh displayed talent from an early age. He remembered a day at the lake, many seasons before. Stubby, strong legs held the child upright; the toddler stumbled only once as he approached his grandfather. Bending his knees, Osh tucked his tiny legs under his body and squatted beside the older man. Too young to appreciate Grandfather's work, the child seemed to understand natural beauty. He stretched his baby fingers toward Grandfather's new stone tool. Grandfather opened his palm and presented the sculpted flint. Little Osh, one hand on his grandfather's bare thigh, ran the chubby fingers of his outstretched hand against the stone touching the sharp, newly cut edges now cradled in the elder's palm.

The clan lived on the shores of the lake which they called Big Waters. At the bottom of the lake, Grandfather thought, there must be hundreds of stones thrown by the children. He threw them himself, as he had seen his father throw for distance and they watched the concentric circles formed from the rocks crashing through the water's surface. As a young boy, Grandfather gathered flat, round scrapers and learned to skip them across the top of the water. In the middle of the lake there must be many good stones for carving as well as a few misplaced scrapers. He never thought of it that way. And this notion brought Grandfather back to the flint stone he now held.

"What do you think, little man? Do you like this new stone?" Before the child could respond, his mother appeared.

"Have food while you indulge this bothersome child," she laughed. She brought her father-in-law dried meat, which he gratefully accepted, and a handful of berries that she placed on a broad leaf beside him. Together, they watched the small boy's awkward steps as he trotted toward the water. On the shore the little one threw rocks, mesmerized by circles expanding on the water's surface.

"One day he will swim like a water snake across the lake to the other shore," his mother ventured.

"One day, he will be a master tool maker," Grandfather

countered. "He will accompany me to gatherings when magic turns the trees to gold and red."

✦ ✦ ✦

Now, years later, Osh was still as inquisitive as ever. "Osh, use your eyes, not your mouth," Grandfather repeated. Every day Osh lingered beside his father and grandfather as they chipped and carved delicate arrows and rounded scrapers. Osh talked all the time, asking questions, telling stories.

"Why is this stone gray, and yours is red?" Osh asked. "Why do you never talk when you are working, Grandfather?" He interrupted. "Why don't the fowl fly as high as the cranes?"

"Pick up a stone and make a tool," from his father. "Follow the lead of your Grandfather," he encouraged. "Use your eyes and not your mouth, Osh," he coaxed.

Osh hovered, waving his arms in great animation as he chatted incessantly beside his father and grandfather while they chipped and carved delicate arrows and rounded scrapers. He talked all the time, asking questions, telling stories. Only Grandfather noticed that while the adolescent babbled, his eyes never left the pounding of each tool; even Osh held his breath as a new stone tool was completed.

They were toolmakers. Sometimes they tapped-out large spears and blades. At other times they honored requests for heavy pounders and stone pestles. He memorized every movement, the flick of the wrist, the directional blow of the implements. In the same way his sister was mentored by their mother's work gathering herbs, curing meat, fetching berries as well as stitching hides.

✦ ✦ ✦

Grandfather's mind wandered, and skipped to the gatherings. Grandfather attended assemblies held each interval when the shoreline and trees beyond turned red, as rich as antelope blood and gold as bright as the sun. His grandson had now attended ten gatherings, his first as a wobbly toddler. That would make him twelve seasons now; twelve times the leaves magically changed colours. Osh interrupted his thoughts.

94

"I can't do this," Osh cried one day when he cracked the end off a nearly perfect point. Osh was passionate about delicate arrowheads. The hunters lashed the fine tips, used for small birds, to thin bamboo shafts. They carved larger arrows for ostrich, turkey, guinea fowl and plains animals.

Grandfather was there. "Try this stone, Osh." He tried again. The young carver stilled; he concentrated on refining another flake of flint. Only then, was the fledgling artist hushed. This time, as he chipped and worked to smooth the edges of the fine point, he worked in silence. Grandfather watched with patience and pride.

Osh was a taut young boy, lean, and fit as a meadow antelope. His tense, striated thighs and elongated calves set him apart as a runner and an athlete. His hair was wiry and unkempt. Sometimes while bathing at the lake, he scooped up a handful of sand and scrubbed his scalp, but not always. His head was a bushy mass.

"Grandfather, did you see my feathers? I got a beautiful bird, but I lost my arrowhead." Osh placed the feathers alongside the spotted feathers of the guinea fowl on his leather quiver. As a rite of passage, young boys hunted small birds, collecting the colourful feathers as trophies on their hide backpacks, symbols of skill.

"I am thrilled with the accuracy of your aim, young Osh," Grandfather encouraged. "You have quite a collection." He fingered the soft quills. "I like the blue and green feathers from the rollers," he continued showing genuine interest. "They are small birds and require a very small arrowhead and great precision." Grandfather was proud of Osh. "You must return to the marsh to locate your arrowhead. You worked hard to carve the flint." With finality he said, "You must locate your arrow for another outing."

"I'll never find it Grandfather," complained Osh.

"Retrace your steps, Son. Remember where your bird fell." Grandfather encouraged, "Look beyond. Always look beyond."

This year grandfather would be esteemed to present his skills at the gathering. This was a great honour for Grandfather and for the clan.

The assemblies, held in the meadow at the edge of the river,

95

encouraged trading, telling stories and gathering news. Walking along the shore they learned of births and deaths since the last meetings. They traded herbs and baskets.

Grandfather and the other wise ones met together several times during the event. He remembered back to other clan meetings with his son and young grandson. Grandfather's heart swelled with pride. His grandson brought new joy to his life. Grandfather and Osh shared a bond that neither explained.

At gatherings, the finest examples were displayed in the arena. Experienced artisans represented each clan. Osh always loved this part, respected all the pieces: baskets woven in different shapes with colours they didn't have in their clan, colours made from tribal dyes of flowers and plant not common along the lake shore; herbs and spices from each region; jewelry made from leather, shells and stones; carry-pieces for food and arrows on hunting trips, and pots made from clays of red and brown and gray earth, sun dried for baking in the open fire.

Osh and the other boys admired the tools; boys and their weapons. He wondered which tool Grandfather would show this time. Or perhaps it would be one of his father's tools. Within their clan there were many carvers. It was a great honour to be selected to display in the arena.

* * *

Grandfather nudged the rock with his calloused foot. "This one's for Osh," he said to no one in particular. He squatted in the soft dirt contemplating the large, bleached flint stone that rested between his leathered feet. With both hands, he gently lifted the stone, turning it over, to look at it from all sides. Grandfather was a toolmaker. His father was a toolmaker; now his son made tools of stone. His young grandson Osh displayed talent from an early age. This stone would make a magnificent implement.

Was Osh ready for this remarkable piece of flint? A master carver would study the stone, view it from all angles before deciding its fate, before deciding its destiny. Grandfather determined that Osh was prepared. Without fanfare, the mentor presented the rough stone.

As a young apprentice, Osh thought carefully about Grandfather's stone. Flint, with all its variations, was Grandfather's favorite stone. This large sand-colored slab would make a fine piece.

As he continued to turn the hardened chunk of earth, a shape began to form in his mind. He knew if he chipped carefully, he would sculpt an efficient tool and one that would give him great pleasure to create. With this flint rock, he had the opportunity to author something beautiful; he saw it as artistic outlet, though he had no word for this, a work of commitment and passion.

He knew also, that if his working tool slipped, or if there was a flaw in the flint stone, the piece, as he now conceptualized it, could be ruined. There were occasions before when his sculpting had not gone as planned. He learned over time to redesign from what was left of the stone, and he had before changed his mind during the process of carving.

By Grandfather's side, Osh observed the position of the rock, the position of the hand and the quickness of the strike that would yield the most efficient results. Perhaps one day he would consider a way to make projectiles travel farther, perhaps by lighter weight and more carefully defined size and shape. But he did not know about future; he only knew about today. And today he, Osh, was concerned with the large flint stone between his hands.

* * *

Osh knew what he would design from Grandfather's stone. Now it was Grandfather's time to watch; he observed with wonder and pride at the young carver's skill.

Osh scanned the tools that surrounded his work place. They were neatly arranged by shape and size. He worked with obsidian, basalt, granite, quartz and different flints. He selected a hammer stone the size of his fist, which he could easily grasp.

With his left hand he gripped the flint stone. He began to strike. The first blow was a success. As the flake fell away, he struck again and a crude shape began to emerge. The first strikes came quickly as he turned the stone over, slicing away at each side until the shape began to form.

He chipped and chiseled carefully, for he knew that other useful tools could be made of smaller flakes. There were chips large enough to fashion arrowheads, leaf blades and perhaps scrapers. The first steps were both the easiest, and the most difficult.

Osh paused at the beauty of this rock that Grandfather gave him to carve. He wanted to be sure that it did not become a pile of shards due to his carelessness.

He was careful too, that he did not create a bulbous formation or ripples, which could, from the force of the blow, alter the larger piece.

Finally, Osh selected a tool to complete the wide blade, for that was what it had now become. This time he chose a long piece of bone. Placing the blade on the ground, Osh steadied the femur, its pointed edge against the flint, and pounded the top of the marrowless, dry bone. By gently twisting the rod, a fluted edge began to emerge as the small chips fell away.

This was Grandfather's stone. Would Grandfather approve of his work? He held the thick shape up to the sun; it was longer than his hand and almost as wide, easy to grip. Grandfather smiled with great pride. He was pleased.

"If I throw it, this blade must be narrow enough to fly through the air," he spoke sitting on his haunches, "if I lance it to a spear or wedge it into a shaft of bone." Thinking out loud he said to Grandfather, "But it must be wide enough to fit in my hand if I need a dagger." The knife took on the elegance of a blade of marsh-grass; a reed along the lake's edge.

When did it happen that Osh carved beautiful arrowheads, and scrapers? One day he was a toddler on the side of the lake, tossing stones into the water, now he carved tools to rival his father and even his grandfather.

Grandfather saw with renewed awareness the brilliance of the stones, the accuracy with which each had been carved. This year, Osh would be by his side at the gathering. They would show their tools together.

"Yes, Osh," Grandfather whispered with pleasure. "Your flint blade must go to the gathering when magic turns the trees to gold and red." He looked beyond Osh as if visualizing the event.

"Your blade will represent our clan in the arena."

With the creation of the blade, Osh came of age as a young carver chosen to display in the arena. For the final feast, utilizing his precious weapon, along with the team of men, he secured the wildebeest to divide amongst attendees to enjoy with wild boar, antelope and hartebeest roasted over open fires as clans chanted and danced until the next season.

Grandfather, now elderly, would not attend another gathering. He would be missed by the other wise men and especially missed by Osh.

Mom Doesn't Do Sick

E veryone in the family knows, Mom doesn't do sick. When the kids were little they knew, if there was no blood or vomit, "Out the door ya go. On to school." No one stayed home for a headache. As a child the only illness I contracted was a rather severe case of measles when I was four.

As an adult, I did acquire a mild case of the mumps and three or four pock marks when the kids contracted the contagious diseases in kindergarten. I was just never sick. When I was young I was lucky. Later I decided I didn't believe in sick. I couldn't rationalize major illnesses like polio, but sickness was a non-issue. Hence my reputation grew.

In Ethiopia we were exposed to all manner of exotic diseases; I never got a one. Finally, while living in the Philippines, Jessica and I came down with dengue fever, a mosquito borne illness. The sheets on the bed felt like needles cutting, slicing across my arms and legs. I finally got a romantic disease.

★ ★ ★

Daryle and I attended a high school performance of "Grease" on Thursday evening at the American School, Paris in Saint Cloud. I was curious how they might portray this story line of teenage promiscuity, conflict and romance. Daryle met with proud parents and I gave high fives to the energetic cast of the American School. We left quickly and barely made the thirty minute drive back to our Paris flat. Daryle shook so much from fever that gripping the steering wheel became difficult; I thought he might need to pull over to the side of the road.

We made it home, parked the car, punched the four digit apartment code, staggered to the elevator, stood in the rattling cage up to the seventh floor and shuffled to our beds without eating. My symptoms were the same. During the day I experienced muscle aches and pains. It must be a virus. I don't do sick, so after a good night's sleep, I would be fine.

In the morning The Mister staggered off to work, back down in l'ascenseur, the rattling cage, with muscle pain, headache and much fever. I dozed off and on during the day and took aspirin to ease the discomfort. That night, again we ate no food and went directly to bed.

The two of us sulked around all weekend with unwelcome lethargy. The flu refused to recede. Still the symptoms did not match up: no vomiting, no diarrhea. Again, we ate nothing. While I consumed aspirin, Daryle continued to devour his daily cocktail of diabetic medication fearful of contradicting pills, all the while both of us sweating through our clothes and soaking our sheets.

"So what do you think's wrong with you?" It was Ian, Skyping from Bangkok to Paris.

"It must be a flu virus," Daryle spoke into the Skype button. "Aches, pain, fever, shaking," they spoke loudly over the connection. "But we should be over it by now," he continued. "I'm wondering," he looked to the side of his desk, then back to the computer screen, "if it might be malaria."

"What?" Ian cocked his head toward the screen and stroked his chin. "No way."

"Well," Daryle paused, "we were there, in Kampala, fourteen days ago," he shifted in his chair, leaning toward the screen. "The incubation period shows up after ten days," he said, "according to the book." He uncrossed his legs under the desk, "That would be about Thursday."

"If you think it's malaria, just get a blood test," Ian said a little too fast. "That will give you the results," he sounded skeptical, "and you can rule it out. You'll know for sure."

By Sunday we needed to get out of the flat, a bit stir-crazy. With no issues of diarrhea or nausea, we rattled down stairs, walked through the lobby, past the concierge and out into the energizing sun. Although *la tour Eiffel* was steps away, it seemed to be kilometers. We felt the energy of the sun. We also felt the drag of our bodies.

The day was *tres speciale*, one of those wacko days: a roller-blade spectacular, a jump off *la tour Eiffel* billed as The Mega-Jump, a distance jump to establish a Guinness World Record. French athletic daredevil, Taig Khris, planned to make an historic jump. The promoters built a platform off the first level of *la tour*.

For several weeks, organizers and promoters advertised the upcoming Mega-Jump. On this day, this *special* day, the crowds grew. French of all ages merged toward *le parc*. Along the *Champ de Mars*, as far as the *Ecole Militaire* newly set-up rollerblade ramps drew the attention of local rollerbladers and skateboarders. Young and not so young boarders flaunted their skills of loop de loops with their blades and boards.

After about an hour walking the promenade along the *Champ de Mars*, waiting for the momentous, record breaking jump, we could tolerate no more. Weak and trembling we felt like losers who could not cope. Like early birds who could not wait for the sunrise, could not wait for the main event, we shuffled toward a bench to people-watch and attempted to wait for the Mega-Jump.

The crowd roared. Taig Khris stood at the top of the ramp waving to the crowd and spoke through a taped-on mini microphone. "*Allooo Pareee!*" Another roar from the crowd. All eyes focused skyward. Children rode their parent's shoulders. Large dogs and small dogs tangled leashes around ankles while cheers from the ground built and encouraged the athlete.

The thirty-four year old thrill seeker roared down the ramp dropping 131 feet from the first floor of the Eiffel Tower landing on his feet of inline wheels and plunging into the foam barriers.

The crowd howled with approval and pleasure.

Exhausted, we clung to each other like the little old couple we had become, and slowly walked back to our flat on Avenue de Suffren, under the serenity of *la tour Eiffel* and crashed into our beds, exhausted from the hour of outdoor exertion.

In the early morning, at double-oh-dark, limping out of bed, Daryle left to send off the 5th graders on their end-of-year class trip. His head pounded and he sweated through his suit and tie. When the school nurse arrived he submitted a blood sample which she sent off to a nearby clinic. She called him within the hour with the results.

⸺ * * * ⸺

The door to the flat opened though it didn't register. Prostrate on my bed, fully clothed, I barely responded to the open door. I dozed. Daryle walked in. "Come on. We're going to the hospital."

"What?" I slurred my words, and rolled over on the bed.

"We're going to the hospital. Get up." He extended his arm to pull me up.

"What?"

"Get up. Malaria. I have malaria. You do too."

I grabbed at my identification papers, keys to the flat and limply followed Daryle down the elevator cage to Michelle's waiting car. Daryle's professional assistant drove us to the American Hospital in Paris.

I expected to receive a shot, a few pills then pop home. Not so. They checked us in like coeds in a frat house. A joint room, a double room, room sharing, a his-her coed room. I had nothing: no toothbrush, hair brush, change of clothes. Nothing. I anticipated a couple of pills and a ride home. They checked us in, few questions asked. It seems we were at risk: older, vulnerable and late to make inquiries or report symptoms, nearly a week after the first indications.

Even in a disheveled state I saw the humour: his and her roller beds. We disrobed and donned designer gowns: matching white, open back, loosely secured with a same-fabric tie leaving the frock to flap. We were too sick to laugh, but I did get it, sort of. We crashed immediately and did whatever they asked of us: pills and tubes. They hooked us up straight away; I fell asleep immediately.

Not sure if I woke up naturally or because someone was exchanging my quinine drip. I looked over at Daryle and thought how vulnerable and silly he looked with a drip bottle hovering over his head and the plastic tube taped to the back side of his hand as if the cylinder might escape.

I looked at my own bed and resting on the white gown, a skinny arm protruded from the truncated sleeve like an unsculpted broom handle, like a brittle piece of uncooked spaghetti. The transparent tube of plastic taped to the back of my hand made me a mirror image of my roommate.

Nurses and doctors floated in and out like French apparitions. I guess it was like any hospital, but I've not spent much time in sanatoriums or rest houses to compare. Both of my babies were delivered in an American hospital in America. I stayed 24 hours. *That* was silly, but we had no money. I endured foot surgery twice in Dubai, again overnight only.

This experience in Paris seemed romantic.

Romantic disease: malaria

Romantic location for the mosquitoes: Kampala.

Romantic city for the illness: Paris.

Romantic roommate: Daryle

Whatever comments the staff made seemed lyrical in French. When they told me I was very sick and very weak, it sounded romantic. They told us we had Malaria Plasmodium Falciparum. *Que romantico! C'est romantique.* The most severe form of malaria, it sounded beautiful.

Daryle, who never once made it through the night without getting up, now fumbled around with his tubes and bottles and drips. I slept intermittently both day and night and watched him slide off the side of the tall hospital bed and shuffle to the loo to relieve his body of the twenty-four hour quinine drips. This was good; all part of the process. Still, I waited, listening for the inevitable crash. Once again, he made it there and back to hike himself up onto the too-high bed.

After three days, they presented us with menus and the food was, well, French; the most passionate food in the world. The cuisine was only sort-of interesting. We still had very little appetite, but I did, at least, recognize the menu. Ah, Paris. There were even wine choices for visitors who might dine with patients.

It seemed a miracle. Thanks to the quinine, the pain started to subside. The British had it right all along, gin with tonic, gin with quinine water. It was the quinine drips that gave us the strength. Oh, we took lots of meds as well. The pain started to subside, but there was still diarrhea and sweating. Daryle's case was complicated because of his diabetes. Anything they gave him in romantic France could be a contradiction to his medications. We needed to get our temperatures down, the sweating stopped and the aching reduced.

For Daryle, hospitalization became a great diet opportunity; an unsolicited occasion to drop those kilos which lingered just slightly over the belt buckle: kilos of cheese and *baguettes*, of crepes and *nouvelle cuisine*: *cassoulet* duck with sausage and white beans; mussels with white wine, Normandy cider, garlic and cream. *Bourguignon* stewed in red wine, *coq au vin* chicken braised in red wine and mushrooms; *escargots* snails baked in their shells with garlic and parsley butter; fish stewed in red wine; *moules a la crem Normande; raclette*, with potatoes, ham, dried beef, even salad *nicoise* with black olives and tuna added weight.

Because of the sugar, he usually avoided desserts of *crem brulee*, éclair, mousse au *chocolat, crepes* or *macaroons*. However, the kilos inched on, the waistline expanded slowly, *un, duex, trois centimètres* at a time.

Now, in the hospital, the weight plummeted. With no appetite, although the infirmary food was French and beautiful, neither of us mustered up any interest. We looked at the menus, yes, we were offered a selection of choices, made a stab at something that might be palatable, but in the end, each day, we couldn't eat. I just pushed the food around on my plate three times a day, a trick I learned from my kids. It was not typical hospital food; I did recognize that. Still, I had no appetite. Nothing looked worthy of consumption. The weight dropped off like loose litter flying off the back of a truck.

On the fourth day, it seemed Jessica showed up. I have no recall of how she came or when, but she appeared in our hospital room.

Jessica: I took a taxi from the airport straight to the hospital and after I had seen you and spoken with the doctor (and visiting hours were over) I took the bus to your flat. I was sort of in transit because I had to go from Dubai to DC for a workshop. You and Dad were very insistent that I sanitize the apartment because someone was coming to look at it.

Jessica made it sound pedantic, however it was the end of the rental contract and the owners announced that they would be dropping in with potential tenants on occasion. Somewhere in the recesses of my subconscious soul I remembered that I was whisked away without considering the possibility of a cup in the sink, a towel in the washer, a hairbrush on the marble vanity.

When she returned to the hospital, Jessica thoughtfully brought our toothbrushes, shampoo and deodorant. She also brought underwear and the nurses confirmed that Daryle could have a razor. With much sensitivity Jessica snatched up some makeup. What's a girl to do?

Jessica: When I spoke to the doctors, I realized they offered two language choices: German and French. I, of course, speak neither. However because I Googled everything there was to know about malaria, the doctors thought I could speak the languages. I just got the gist of it all. Plus, one just knows what hospital routines are like.

Was it the medication or the illness? We couldn't hear. Our beds were less than two meters apart and we couldn't hear each other. We weren't strong enough to stand up and walk around the room and I didn't realize we were shouting. Daryle was concerned about an upcoming board meeting and he wanted to talk through some issues. I couldn't hear him and he could not hear my responses.

"The last board meeting is tomorrow," he mumbled. "I should be there."

"What did you say?" I asked vaguely aware of a pending dialogue.

"WHAT?" he muttered back at me.

"What did you just say?" I now projected, rolling on my side toward his bed.

"I should- be- at- the- final- board meeting."

"Terrible timing," I offered.

"What?" I think he mumbled again. **"I can't hear you,"** he sounded exasperated.

Jessica: You and Dad couldn't hear each other and kept asking me to stand between your beds and relay messages. I tried not to laugh my head off. You were both shouting.

After six days, the doctors concurred we were ready for release. Michelle, Daryle's assistant, came to translate the paperwork and help expedite exit procedures. Cured. Home-Free, as they say. We were ready and eager to return to our Paris flat under *la tour Eiffel*.

Cured, if not healthy, we sorted and counted out a cocktail of pills. We each needed handfuls of tablets several times a day. Jessica helped us tally the combination. It seemed confusing, and I couldn't wrap my head around it. For Daryle, it was a balance, a contradiction with his diabetes medication. We sat at the kitchen nook counting pills. It seemed I required ten in the morning, five at noon and three before bed, something like that. Daryle's regime was more complicated. Jessica sorted it out.

Ian arrived at five o'clock in the morning from Bangkok. How he arranged that I will probably never know. An hour later he punched our apartment key-pad and we buzzed him up to the flat. The joy of having our son and daughter in Paris resonated in a brilliant and priceless manner. This was not a summer holiday. They came out of compassion, at the sacrifice of their families at the stressful end of their school calendars in Dubai and

Bangkok. They came because, although we didn't realize it, we needed them.

We spent two days as a normal family enjoying picnics under la tour Eiffel. It was not normal. We pretended. We dragged our picnic of bread and cheese and wine, tossed a blanket to enjoy the ambience under la tour and pretended it was a regular family picnic. It was not.

Although released from the hospital, and the French paperwork claimed we were cured, we were stressed, anxious and weak, not sick but not well. Whether it was the malaria or the lack of food or the lack of exercise or a combination of all three, we felt frail.

"Thanks for coming Jessica," I hugged her as she prepared to head on to workshops in the US. "I guess we were pretty hopeless," I smoothed my sweater, luxuriating in my own clothes.

"You were awesome, Mom," she said grasping the handle of her roll-on bag. "You rock," she grinned. "You were the classiest American in the place," she looked at her dad, "followed by Dad." Then added, "If you're going to get an exotic disease," she said running her fingers through her thick head of hair. "I'm glad it was in Paris." She looked at her brother, "Thank god we didn't have to head out to Ouagadougou," again consulting her brother. "We might not have bothered." She tucked her hair behind her ear. "Hey. Paris is Paris," and she headed out the door. "I'm just sayin."

When released from the hospital I thought we were cured. Actually, we were released from the IV tubes. Ian stayed another week to help us build up strength and cultivate appetites. He started by taking us, escorting us, on short walks a half block to the vegetable market operated by Arabs. I appreciated those men. They always seemed pleased when I used Arabic in the shop. In a few days we walked to la Tour Eiffel and back. We walked along the Seine, later across to the Trocadéro as our strength improved.

In the flat, Ian prepared diners, three course meals including salad, entre, cheese and fruit. He mopped the small floor of the kitchen, Swiffered the hardwood floors and Hoovered the carpets. Who knew? After years of nagging, before he flew off to boarding school, I was delighted if he picked up his socks. Now I learned that he did know how to cook and clean.

He helped Daryle get back to work in small increments, a couple of hours at a time, driving to Saint-Cloud while his father attempted to catch up. End of the year scenarios, union meetings, culminating projects, final exams, reports, teacher meetings, parent meetings clamored for attention. The same was true for Ian, school Principal, who left Bangkok where he, too, should have been winding down the end of the school year.

Ian took us back to the American Hospital for a final follow-up. We sat in the hallway awaiting our appointments and the definitive *"Oui, tres bien,"* or whatever they would tell us.

"Bonjour," the doctor spoke through his nose. He looked first at me, then at Daryle. *"Comment allez-vous?"* he asked. This was about the extent of my French conversational skills.

"Bien, merci," I mumbled, hoping the dialogue would switch to English. He rattled off something and I answered, "Excuse me?"

"Ah," he said looking down at the charts. Or was he looking down his nose? "How are you feeling now?"

"Much better, *merci,*" I spoke for both of us. "We are getting our strength back," I looked uncomfortably at my hands. "We appreciate the care and attention we received," I said running my thumb along the strap of my designer bag, "the care from the hospital staff."

"Bon," he snapped the file closed and stood up. *"Au revoir,"* he said thrusting out his hand.

We never saw the doctors or the hospital again. *"Au revoir* to you too, malaria."

Mom doesn't do sick. Mom does exotic diseases. No blood, no vomit. Therefore, Mom only sort-of did sick: exotic sick.

Trouble with Politics

The trouble with this country was the politics. That is, I had trouble with the politics. It was still not what I thought. I needed to write it out to figure out what I thought, balanced with what I knew, with what I was learning. We traveled from Islamabad, Pakistan. We landed in Johannesburg, flew to Cape Town and rented a car. We traveled from Joburg to Cape Town to Port Elizabeth to somewhere north, beyond Queenstown. The green, pastoral countryside played host to cattle and sheep and fenced-in ostrich lurking on large farms.

We planned to travel to Iran for the holidays, our holidays not theirs. Two days before our departure date they cancelled our visas. Again. We have often come close to traveling there but in the end, always the visas were denied. The hotels were all full, there was a conference going on, there was a political issue of the week but primarily we were denied because we carried American passports. There must be a face saving device that prevents the clerical people from saying, "No, I'm sorry, we don't entertain American tourists." Two days later we flew instead to South Africa.

Apartheid ended in February last year, 1994, four years after the release of Nelson Mandela. Arrested for sabotage, he spent twenty-seven years in prison. At the time he said, "I do not deny that I planned sabotage. I did not plan it in a spirit of recklessness nor because I have any love of violence. I planned it as a result of a calm and sober assessment of the political situation that had arisen after many years of tyranny, exploitation and oppression of my people by the whites."

Now, just ten months later, it was December, the seasons flipped from the northern hemisphere. We drove through a fierce 'summer' hail storm. I wondered if the rented car was dented. I thought the windshield might crack; the stones smacked against the glass and roof and hood.

I tried to understand how the country thought. They, the whites, didn't like hearing that things looked much better than they did twenty years ago when we first visited. A Swiss gentleman, with the unlikely name of Archie, and his white South African wife ran the Bed-and-Breakfast where we spent the night.

We reveled in a day trip from the B-and-B to the celebrated wine country in Stellenbosch. We drove through hectares of lush green vineyards. The grapes, burgundy, purple and blue dangled like clusters of jewels fit for royalty. Suspended from trellises, they hung like unwrapped presents tempting us to stop and snatch them up.

Opposite the vineyards, manors dotted the road. By random selection, and they all were beautiful, we stopped for a picnic lunch at a winery estate. We swirled, sniffed, sipped and sampled reds and whites, selected a bottle for lunch, then purchased a gourmet picnic box. The lunch included a *charcuterie* board, my first time to learn the French term for a selection of cured sausages, bacon, prosciutto, pate and a bit of chutney.

The picnic included baguettes, cheese selections, smoked trout pate, farm salad, beetroot and feta salad, spinach and feta quiche, marinated olives and a pastry selection. Pinotage, a red South African blend was popular but too sweet for our taste. We selected a signature Cabernet Sauvignon and lounged on the grounds for a leisurely and elegant box lunch. A 'chic-nic,' as they say, on the lawns under drooping willow trees.

Archie greeted us in the drive as he tossed a Frisbee to his South African ridgeback. He wanted to talk and the rapport felt mutual. We wanted to hear and he craved conversation. I could almost feel how he tried to wrap his head around the new South African conundrum.

"We sent our daughter to London this year to get work," he started as he attempted to tell us the real situation in his country. "They tell us," he invited us into the sitting room, "They tell us white kids can't go to college even with the best scores," he leaned forward in the upholstered chair, "because black students must be given priority." He looked at Daryle knowingly.

We listened. We were his audience, an audience of western listeners. He wanted us to know, to hear it from the white Afrikaner, though he was Swiss, a longtime resident, perhaps of dual citizenship. And we were eager to hear his perspective.

"I would tolerate a black family or two moving into the neighbourhood," he ran his fingers through his thick head of hair. "Not next door," he looked boldly at Daryle, "and certainly not to be included in my home."

Archie, made no bones about not wanting to live with coloureds or work with them. With his upbringing, he admitted, there was no way he could or would change his attitude. He searched for the word. "You Americans have a word for it, where they work out quota systems."

"It's called affirmative action," Daryle said.

"Yeah. That's it," he nodded. "We're starting to get some of that here." And then he told us a story that seemed to summarize his thoughts, his philosophy.

"There was this tall, bright, black woman. She stayed with us for three months." We leaned in. "She was speaking at all the universities and to the senate and with the politicians."

I was not sure where this was going or why he articulated this to us. "She was very intelligent telling everyone how to go about setting things up for the blacks and how to work through our transition."

I was not sensitive to how recent this so-called end of apartheid was, how contemporary the concept must have seemed having been decreed just ten months earlier; how much of an educated effort it might require. For me, it was a non-issue. Okay, finally it's mandated. Apartheid is now illegal. Of course it would take time; I was not that naïve. Having lived all over the world, so to speak, I did not, however, relate to the difficulty of this mandate.

Archie continued. "One day she left town. Just vanished," he said. "No one heard from her and she left everyone high and dry with bills to the airlines, the colleges, the shops, restaurants." He looked at Daryle then at me. "She ran up thousands of rand in debts and took off." He folded his hands in his lap, cocked his head and looked out the window. "That was the last we heard from her," he said staring into space.

He already explained where the 'coloureds,' "we call them that because they are all mixed," lived on the other side of the highway. We saw their homes with aluminium roofing, covering wooden boxes or cardboard.

"They just came in today to do their shopping before the stores close for the holidays." He was matter of fact. "Most of the farmers in this dorp," he looked at me for understanding, "that's what we call a city," then continued, "most of the farmers will be closing up their homes and heading for their beach houses for the holidays." He added, "They give their workers a day off too." He said this as if this was a generous gesture, which tells me blacks do not live in white residential areas.

* * *

On the large, wood plank kitchen table I noticed a hefty pottery bowl heaped with mushrooms the size of soccer balls.

"Wow! Look at those mushrooms," I nearly yelped, inappropriately American.

"You like mushrooms?" Archie asked.

"We love mushrooms. Like fer shure," I turned on the California talk.

"These are wild," he informed us. "I collect them from the forest," he beamed, "a few miles from the house." Then, "Would you like some for breakfast?"

"That would be awesome," more California talk. My mouth watered at the thought.

True to his word, the Swiss South African Archie sautéed a pan full of sliced wild mushrooms, grilled lightly in butter with a hint of garlic. Each slice measured the diameter of the plate. He arranged them on a huge platter, staggered like stair steps. It was almost too beautiful to disrupt.

In another cast iron pan he sautéed onion, strips of ham, bacon, tomato chunks and added the dark diced mushroom stems. He whipped up a dozen eggs with rich cream, gently poured them into the pan and layered the entire ensemble with fresh, shaved parmesan. Peeking through the fluffy pale eggs, the dark mushrooms highlighted the mixture promising added flavor and texture. When cooked through, he sliced the deep dish and served it up in pie shaped wedges to consume before we headed on.

I thought of Archie and all the Archies of South Africa as they worked through their South African transition.

* * *

We enjoyed the morning at Addo Elephant Park one hour outside Port Elizabeth. The exhilaration of being in the car, thermos of hot coffee, cameras and binoculars ready was as comforting as a security blanket is to a toddler. Elephant roamed the area like raffle-ticket sellers at a gala. In front of cars, sometimes between cars, they ruled the road. Abundant in number and in size they wandered the park. But I avoided the thoughts I wanted to address.

* * *

On Christmas Eve we still drove. It was five pm, yet the sun was high in the sky, to set after eight pm. It didn't seem like Christmas Eve but we would fabricate something, some-thing. I did bring Christmas Eve pajamas for sweet dreams and candy canes that I put in the cocktail glasses for starters. I also brought caviar and purchased a recommended local white wine. But that's about it. No traditional clam chowder, as Daryle liked to prepare. On the coast we might have had a chance, but as it stood, we didn't even have a room.

Due to our spontaneous decision to fly to South Africa, we made no reservations for rooms along the way, maintaining only a vague idea of an itinerary. We rented the car at the airport then headed out. *Que sera, sera.* We ended up at a family resort. Christmas Eve at a popular family overnight spa. Kids ran, screeched and giggled jumping into the pool, climbing out dripping, hair clinging to their heads, reaching for towels. A jolly Santa roamed the grounds tossing candies from a skinny red bag ho, ho, ho-ing around the grounds. Merry Christmas to all, and to all a good night.

Bungalows, Estates and New Year's Resolutions

Getting into Swaziland was easy compared to crossing other African borders.

Park the car, get out and enter a wooden shack.
Show passports.
From behind the counter, bam, bam, bam.
Three inky stamps utilize two and a half passport pages.
Get back into the car and exit South Africa.

Drive five meters to the next bungalow.
Get out of the car.
Show passports.
Pay road tax.
Get visa, bam, bam, bam another two pages of stamps.
Reenter the car and enter Swaziland.

We meandered north through unheard-of towns and villages. The road through Swaziland felt more African, unlike the big cities of Johannesburg and Cape Town. The area seemed rural. Though inappropriate to judge a country from the front seat of a car, I felt a sense of traditional Africa.

The registration at Hlane Royal National Park proved more pedantic than entering the country. The man at the office meticulously wrote down numbers, adding, re-adding, entering statistics into a log, preparing receipts in triplicate, issuing stamps, requesting Daryle to sign a registry book, requiring minute superfluous data. We paid the fees at last, standing under a sign that read, "Warning: Poaching in Swaziland is a jailable offence."

Inside the park, the roads stuck to the tires like teeth held in caramel candy. "Don't drive around today, Sir," someone hollered from the bungalow-office. "Too much muddy."

We tossed our bags inside the simple self-catering rondavel and pulled up plastic chairs on the deck to enjoy a cool drink. For lunch I dug around in the cooler to find a sharp cheese, freshly baked brown bread and a huge avocado which I halved and accented with a twist of coarse ground salt and pepper.

Ostrich roamed the grounds like a flock of Big Birds from Sesame Street. A family in the park prepared barbequed sausage over an open fire. The father was white, mother mixed, four children were mixed with dominant black genes, and the daughter's teenage friend was darker black. Was this acceptable in Swaziland, were they South African? Were these the colored's of whom Archie spoke? We spent the afternoon reading. The roads never did dry up.

Daryle suffered from a bout of gout. Was it diet, stress, physical condition, or all of the above?

We slipped into Krueger National Park for an overnight. The following day he was so tired driving out of Kruger, I wasn't sure he could make it. He yawned and yawned grasping the wheel with both hands.

"Do your gout pills make you drowsy?" It seemed like conversation might be helpful.

"No," but he had been taking the pills for several days. "I didn't sleep last night."

"I didn't sleep either," I said. I bent my knee and raised my foot to the seat. "I think it was the air-con in the small banda," I started to get angry. "That thing went on and off all night. I was either sweating like crazy or freezing." I swiveled toward him, "Plus we were up at five a.m. for the game drive. No wonder you are yawning."

"Seeing those lionesses hunkered in the grass and walking in the bushes," he said, "there were six. And then they decided to walk across the road in front of the car."

"That made Kruger worthwhile, but we sure didn't see much else," I added.

December thirtieth and 1995 would soon end. We headed west toward the fishing area in the mountains. There were no accommodations. Even along the mountain roads, No-vacancy signs hung over Welcome signs. Everything looked fully booked for New Year's Eve. The rural towns offered nothing. The few hotels and motels along the road announced no space. By chance we saw a sign for Walkersons Estates, a private lane. The moment we turned onto the long winding road overlooking the beautiful valley of cultivated crops and ponds with a clean river and forested hillsides I could feel the heart palpitations from Daryle, eager to wet a line in the pristine water. The front seat vibrated.

When we reached Walkersons Estates the discussion in the car began. We pulled into the drive. Who would go in to the reception desk to ask about a room? I did have on relatively clean clothes which I saved for Kruger in case we hung out around the lodges. I mustered up my courage and walked to the reception of the handsome lodge.

"I'm looking for information about your place," I said to the woman at the front desk. "We were driving by and saw your sign." I looked down at my dusty feet. "Would you have a brochure?"

"Oh yes," she smiled ignoring my disheveled look. After days of camping and rough safari we knew our state of grubbiness. We never noticed while amongst campers. Yet here in the luxurious world of estate dwelling we suddenly sensed our campfire look; our safari grunge.

"And would you have any rooms for this evening?" I felt like a worm.

"We have just one lakeside cottage left. It's only available for one night because it is reserved for New Year's Eve. I think it is waiting for you." She was amiable, accommodating and as gentle as a high school counselor assisting a distraught teenager.

"What are your prices?" I asked as I looked beyond the reception to the open wine gallery and bar, not daring to take in the sitting area.

"The price is 480R per person," this was a bit above our budget, "with dinner and breakfast included plus any fishing equipment you need, game drives, and it includes full use of the facilities for hiking."

"Well, thank you very much," I glanced down at the brochure.

"Do you want to talk with your husband?" she noticed I didn't pull out my credit card.

"Yes, thanks, and either he will see you in a few minutes or we'll never see you again." I laughed and she returned the laughter. "He is interested in fishing."

* * *

It was all so civilized. Premier trout fishing in an exquisite setting. What set it apart was the attention to detail. We were made to feel welcome from the minute I enquired at the front desk. The cottages stood beautifully appointed with two heavy armchairs facing a stone fireplace, which the staff lighted during dinner. Beside the bedside lamps the reading included hardback coffee-table books on fishing, country life in the eighteen hundreds and a novel about living with forest animals and their antics.

On the ottoman between the chairs in front of the fire were three magazines, one on fishing and two on lifestyles. A picture of Mouna al Rashid's *Lady Moura* launched in Monaco graced one of the pages. The bath included a separate shower with a clear glass door, the fixtures white with gold and, luxury upon luxury, a toilet *and* a bidet.

The soap was tied with a tartan plaid bow as was the extra roll of toilet paper. The folded face cloths wore tartan bows placed atop like young girls dressed for the dance. Shampoo, liquid bath soap and lotions carried Breck labels.

Every day we discussed what we heard and what we thought we learned, trying to make sense of the country. A professor we met at the estate talked to us about his work at one of the universities. He and his colleagues were mandated to take black students who did not, according to his assessment, want to be there. They did not want to be there to learn. We already knew that Archie's daughter was not allowed to register as a new student. It almost seemed to be apartheid in reverse.

"The students sit there, slouched," he smirked as he spoke. "They extend their legs out from under their desks and just sit there with blank faces." The professor looked at Daryle, "They have no understanding of the lectures." He continued, "When they don't get it, they streak through the campus and physically rip it apart."

But did the white professor want the students to succeed? Something in his rhetoric led me to believe he desired, wanted to prove they were incompetent. Did he think, 'you can lead a horse to water but can't make him drink?' Perhaps the staff needed training during this transition, skills to bring these non-eager students up to speed.

That evening with other guests, we sipped white wine from narrow glasses around a massive stone fireplace which roared from the logs like a lion in the park. The bottle, our private stock, rested in a chilled wine room off the lounge. Attentive servers hovered out of sight.

What would be our New Year's resolutions, our affirmations for the upcoming year in Pakistan? In some ways the work in Islamabad provided more stressors than other schools. Parents from various communities came to the city directly from central casting, as Daryle liked to say. A moderately influential senior student claimed he was a eunuch. Who would check? Thank god I was not the school nurse. US embassy personnel expressed reason to be nervous for security issues; a huge bomb left a crater 10 meters wide at the Egyptian embassy, four blocks from our house and the city waffled under the strong leadership of Benazir Bhutto and her husband, Mr. Ten Percent.

Daryle and I focused our affirmations on professional development. I needed to complete papers and two more online courses before taking the summer onsite classes for my Master's. Daryle's affirmations dealt with more edu-babble though he also wanted to get in better shape. We suffered no regrets for 1994/1995 in Pakistan and looked forward to the upcoming year.

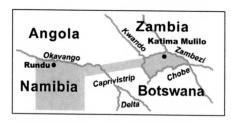

Twisted

The horrible sand road out of Chobe required high speed, four-wheel drive, and led to lots of sliding and shifting and bouncing. The food catapulted out of the cooler, boxes smashed, and juice and milk squirted everywhere; the wine box disintegrated, though we did save the wine. The boiled eggs shelled themselves, the boiled potatoes smashed to mashed.

After traveling a southern African circuit around Zimbabwe, Namibia and Botswana we needed to cross the Caprivi Strip from Botswana back to Namibia. The strip, often the scene of conflict, borders Zambia, and Angola to the north. From where we were in Botswana the only way to get into Namibia was via the dubious Caprivi Strip.

Our convoy included ten to twelve vehicles, all four-wheel drive. Several semi-trucks and open trucks filled with soldiers led the procession; other bile coloured machines snaked in and out between *l'assemblage*.

We started single file across a bridge then stopped at gunshot. What? The soldiers fired across the hills. It scared the bejeebers out of me. We left without the soldiers, or at least those firing. The travel speed seemed about 90 to100 kilometers per hour. An army truck sped by waving to us to close it up. We left at 9am sharp Zimbabwe time, 8am Namibia time and the travelers included commuters, tourists and campers. We closed up, but moved slower, staying at 100 kph. It should take two hours at this pace.

A military truck patrolled back and forth speeding up then dropping back keeping an eye on the convoy. Just as I thought *remain attentive, you can't relax*, Daryle put in a Rock and Roll tape. It didn't help. It was one way traffic; we felt like sitting ducks. 'Wonder where the bad guys are? I looked around like a secret service employee on sniper duty. It seemed to me as if they, the bad guys, were on Daryle's side of the car, his side of the road: the Angolan side of the strip. Silly thought. One problem of course, was poverty. No one, the government in particular, funded the rebel groups; robbery was a big factor, publicity another.

From the start I tensed about this drive. Not concerned about our lives, I only cared about our possessions. Twisted. Shortage and scarcity were an issue. For security reasons you can't ship valuables thus I hand-carried jewelry, three computers, passports, cameras and binoculars and considerable cash. Good grief. Not sure what I was thinking: rather be dead than surrender my valuables? I must be warped in my thought process. We ended up once again in transition from one country, this time Pakistan, en route to another life, another country, albeit America.

Thirty minutes into the drive, and all remained uneventful. The grassy terrain appeared yellow for lack of rain. Immature trees off to the side of the road left gaps in the landscape which allowed for wide visibility. I scanned the area like a vigilante looking through the faux forest trying to ferret out the foe.

Every few kilometers a sign pointed toward the town of Divundu, but little else along the road indicated any suggestion of community. I looked out the car window toward the end of the convoy; there was not even a tiny cluster of round housing *tukuls* to give a semblance of normalcy to the strip. I even wished for an offensive advertising sign; anything to indicate life. Not so. Ironically, littered along the roadside like Burma Shave jingles, the only signs posted 'Danger: Elephant.' Incongruous. We saw no animals, not even a squirrel.

One hour into the trip I replaced the Super-Gold-Rock-'N-Roll tape, recorded from the radio, with a Windham Hill sampler. It doesn't matter if you have heard it before; you can never remember any of the elevator music. It soothed. Along the side of the road I noted patches of grass fires burned black. I wondered if gunfire acted as the starter.

Halfway into the trip, the convoy stopped. All the soldiers leaped off the olive green ferries, which hosted mounted machine guns, and bounded for the bushes. As if on cue, all the men drivers turned off the ignitions. They, with the male passengers, headed for the woods. Big heads, small bladders. After five to eight minutes we took off again and reached the end of the strip in just under two hours.

The village at the turnoff to Popa Falls teemed with pea soup green and brown camouflage attire. A parking area housed fifteen official bile coloured vehicles. The uniformed police waved us through and we were on our own. Several cars in the front of our convoy turned off for petrol. We sped ahead. Although the road was paved and fairly well maintained, it was still tense driving. We needed to get to Grootfontain for the evening, then head for Etosha tomorrow. We did not see one animal in the Caprivi National Park. Everything was gone. The signs for Elephant were a charade. There were no animals left. All were gone, hopefully migrated out of the conflict zone.

We got through the strip. No one shot our tires out. No one stole the computers or cash, nor the cameras or binoculars. We were not kidnapped.

The Written Word

A thousand words is worth a picture. This is how it seems with Africa. I'm struck with the visitor's need, mine included, to capture the moment on Fuji. Fumbling around with settings, lenses, moving the car, adjusting this and that, juggling cameras we aim for the perfect shot before the animal darts into the shrub. We spend so much time *capturing* the moment that we can't savour it until we develop the film a month later. Even with a digital camera, we can't download until we return to our desktops back home, wherever that is.

The value of the written word is that while my eyes absorb the action, my fingers act as an extension of the brain transcribing the details to print. I think through my fingers; I sit and absorb the scene at the water hole with no distractions.

Guinea fowl peck their way to the water picking up bits of grain and bugs, their flat, square shape preventing them from distant flight. Gazelle prance in, heads held high in family units of bucks and harems, while zebra take their time ambling to the water, munching grass, going back before going forward to the water. Marabou stork glide in and wade about the edges, not unlike the water birds of Florida. My transcripts mean more to me than any of my photos.

We waited against the African skyline on the edge of the Okavango swamps and deltas; we waited for the elusive elephant to water. The forests, badly damaged from these pachyderms, exhibited uprooted, knocked over trees some split mid-trunk, many dead or dying. Abundant animal sign on the roads, soft, sandy not well maintained roads, indicated large numbers of game throughout Moremi Park in Botswana, north.

Still we waited.

The elephants did not come, and driving around we did not find them. Back at camp we set a fire and enjoyed anchovies on crackers and sipped tin cups of Tanqueray. We sat around the sparkling flames like crones waiting for the pot to boil and heard the elephants. Close enough to hear but still in the distance as they broke branches and trashed the trees from afar. We hoped they would walk through our campsite. Eventually, the sounds drifted off and the elephants with them. We climbed into our treetop lodge above our camper jeep.

★ ★ ★

"Helloh. How ah you?" The Savuti gate guard wanted my Alphasmart three battery hand held computer. He really wanted it. Wanted to have my address to get one and he will send me money. He has given us the site quietly and no one should know about it because we were not booked in advance. What kind of security is this? Close to the gate. Big elephant in the grounds next to us. If the elephant don't get us the bandits, the corruption will.

We climbed into our treetop lodge atop the truck. I read Margaret Attwood's strange book *Blind Assassin* for 45 minutes.

A novel within a novel; within 600 pages of a novel and a Booker Award this year. It is bizarre. Strange.

At one in the morning I heard it. Maybe the noise was a fox in the trash, or more threatening, someone trying to get into the truck. The only thing we left out was a case of water. I hoped. Daryle stopped breathing too. I whispered, "There's something out there."

He whispered back, "The only thing we left out is the water, right?"

"Yeah. It's something big."

"Yeah." Silence. We did not breathe. My eyes wide open, I saw nothing inside the darkened tent. But I heard everything.

A branch pulled off the tree.

Pods fell to the ground.

Thump, thump of silent pads

stepped closer to our car and tent-on-the-roof.

Salvador Dali
and Sleeping Bully

Before we reached Grootfontein we paused slightly off-road at a mud hole. A bachelor-group of elephants milled around the murky, shallow pond.

I pulled out the Elephant Joke Book. "How can you tell the difference between an elephant and a grape?" I read from page one.

Daryle looked sideways at me.

"Grapes are purple," I read from the book. "Okay," I said, "what's the difference between an elephant and grass?" I answered myself, "They're both green, except the elephant."

"Are you through?" Daryle asked.

A large mammoth stood in the centre of the pond cooling his heels. Knee-deep, he churned the water making a huge splash, creating waves and agitating the grey mud until it covered his belly. With his front foot he forced the water back in a pawing motion: time to cool off with a mud bath.

"Now," I said as we watch the antics, "how can you tell the difference between a grape and an elephant if you›re colorblind?" Who makes up these jokes I wondered? "Dance on it for a while. If you don›t get any wine, it›s an elephant."

Daryle rolled his eyes.

"What did the grape say when the elephant stood on it?" I was on a roll. "Nothing, it just let out a little whine." Arg. We had been in the car too long.

A second behemoth relaxed on his knees resting, cooling his belly. A third stood drinking the churned-up mud, like kids guzzle chocolate milk, then also knelt down and rolled over on his side. A fourth dropped down with slow determination, like the New Year's pendulum at Times Square, then rolled in the thick, grey mud with the fraternity of males.

Two young bachelors, an adolescent and a younger bull, pushed each other back and forth, head to head, on the far side of the hole. As the two bulls sparred, the mud-bath king, the Sleeping Bully stood up to reveal himself as the largest elephant at the hole. He syphoned more water through his droopy proboscis to blow it, spray it, over his glazed body. He kneeled back down and showing great dexterity rolled over nearly on his back, displaying great agility for his size.

Images of Salvador Dali elephants pranced through my mind depicting an incongruous image: massive bodies supported by spindle legs, birdlike twigs, the antithesis of power, strength and dominance; the essence of lightness, floating across the sky.

Sleeping Bully churned the water with his feet in the center of pond as he swallowed the slushy substance. Muck caked over his eyes; it must feel-so-good. He flapped his mud encrusted ears, turned back and forth, kneeled down and actually crawled forward on his knees. Sleeping Bully would sleep well this night if only for short periods. He got up, slid down and stood again, climbed out of the waterhole splashing, displacing litres and litres, gallons and gallons of water from this mud pit in the ground.

Ready for sundowners, we sat around our small fire, Daryle like a film director in his safari chair. He held out his tin cup like a beggar at the mission. I opened the scotch and decanted a bit, but I couldn't resist one final spurious witticism from the Elephant Joke Book.

"Why don›t elephants drink martinis?" I asked.

Daryle just looked at me.

"Have you ever tried to get an olive out of your nose?"

Badonkadonk In The Making

We moved to Mumbai after the sudden death of the headmaster in August, 2003, just before the opening of the school year. In three weeks we shut down our US house, prepaid our US bills and packed eight suitcases. By necessity, the adjustment to Mumbai was quick. Preplanning a trip or a job is a luxury. We jumped into India like Alice tumbled down the rabbit hole.

Mumbai is confrontational: in your face. It assaults all your senses, simultaneously, day by day, festival by festival. We arrived in August at the start of the festival of Ganesh.

Ganesh takes the form of a corpulent man with an elephant head, four arms and two chubby legs. He is the representation of renewal, restart, beginning anew: the god of wisdom and knowledge. To the community, our arrival seemed symbolic. This was good, but not the fat legs part.

Mumbai: the armpit of India, some said. That's not to say there aren't wonderful people nestled close inside the pit. Those we met, colleagues, parents and friends showed us the potential of India, but poverty prevails. Overwhelming dearth is in your face, not as tragedy but as fact.

I loved Mumbai, the festivals, the colours, the cows in the streets, the movie-making in the roads. But this day, this week, I needed to be away from the crowds, and every street, shop, walkway was a crowd. Kenya provided tranquil therapy.

———————— ⋆ ⋆ ⋆ ————————

"Jambo, Sir," Jambo-George extended his arm in warm greeting. "Jambo, Mama," he pumped my hand a bit rough, full of enthusiasm. I appreciated the respectful title, Mama. "Welcome back." His grin spread across his face. Six o'clock in the morning and the airport bustled as he tossed our luggage into the van.

Bernard would again be our driver. Oh joy: translate that not as oh goodie, rather as oh great, oh no, oh well. We knew Bernard from a previous trip to Kenya.

As we bumped along driving from Nairobi to Tsavo East, although we viewed game within thirty minutes of leaving the airport, thoughts of India embedded my mind. I thought, Mumbai is just a street away from hovels and slums. A festival every day; a Bollywood movie-in-the-making every week, in the centre of the road, or just off to the side, causing rubberneck delays.

In Kenya, looking across the sculpted land, across to the hillsides, I realized how sharp and clear the features of the geography. Each shrub along the hillside rock face was crystal clear: pristine air, how unlike Mumbai. No pollution. No slum fires, no plastic bags floating down open sewers. No filthy, matted-hair beggars pounded on the window of the car when we stopped. Clean unspoiled air, polluted only by the sweet tobacco aroma of Daryle's pipe. No ugly black crows soared overhead, challenging, daring. Instead, glossy black hornbills walked along the side of the road like prima donnas waiting to go on stage; red and blue rollers streaked across the sky.

We drove five hours to the tented camp. The road was not bad, just long. Minutes out of Nairobi we sighted a herd of giraffe, a large group of twenty or twenty-five. Once inside the park we observed water buck, baboons and families of elephant before our arrival in time for lunch.

The camp site seemed relaxed with a comfortable ambiance. Still, we were advised to leave no valuables, ever; always carry any valuables. Most tourists carried cameras, phones, pads and pods and binoculars. Because we were in transition, leaving Mumbai, heading to the US, we carried computers; I think we lugged four between us, plus my important jewelry, not meant for safari, and legal documentation required for reentry. Our safari clothes were tacky khaki basic. If someone took them, they needed them more. The large tent included a private water closet and cold shower; no lock; a tent with a zipper.

The substantial lunch was too much main course. A watered-down broth preceded the weighty rice entree. The starchy carb would soon be measurable in the form of a developing badonka-donk. Red wine saved the meal and helped us relax after the tension of the drive. While I pondered the potential of developing a huge *puet*, backside, I wondered why so many of the world's rice-eaters are thin.

Sitting at a nearby table we overheard, with no difficulty, an American family discussing their trip with the Kenyan guide.

"Yes, I'm doing research to compare Muslim and Christian attitudes toward the AIDS virus." My soup spoon stalled mid-air at this research topic. "Yes," she started her second sentence also in the affirmative. "I want to convert the Muslim women." I could not swing around to get a glance at the author of this speech. No response from the guide. Her over-loud, jolly, chirpy voice continued.

"You know," she said with authority, "Muslim men want women covered," she did not slow down, "because women are provocative," this was juicy, "or something." I could only imagine the captive guide. "It's the men's problem," I knew where this was going, "because they have no control," she paused, "of their emotions." Every other sentence someone in the family said 'American' this or 'American' that. How embarrassing. "We're Mormon." I didn't hear the guide's response, then she said, "It's like Christian, but it's Mormon." Then she added, "No! It's not Catholic at all." When they left their table we watched a well fed family of four shuffle across the camp.

Later in the afternoon, prime viewing time, Daryle said, "Let's head out for game viewing." He adjusted his baseball cap; so American. "You ready?" He slung his backpack over his shoulder and headed toward the van. The binoculars hanging from his neck bounced off his chest like a rubber ball attached to a paddle. He sat in the front with Bernard. I sat in the second row of seats with my gear.

Daryle twisted around to confirm that I was organized to head out. "Holy Cow," he said, shaking his head. "Look at you," his arm rested on the back of his seat as he gawked at me. "You look like you have your entire office suite," he said as much for Bernard as for me. "Computer, binoculars," he called out the items like reading from a checklist. "Digital camera, water." It was true. Because we shared the van with no one, we enjoyed the space. Everything lined up at my fingertips, with a thermos of coffee wedged between my feet like a cylinder in a vice.

No animals. Wherever they were before, they were not there now. They moved on. We moved on.

For dinner the staff served deep-fried bream, too much crispy, too much oil, and not-so-fluffy white rice, too much starchy; the better to sport a customary backside. Again proof I would soon be endowed with a traditional badonkadonk, ba donk a donk, a larger-than-life behind esteemed and prized in some cultures.

After dinner, we gathered at the campfire for a fireside talk. The program for the evening was a story about the Masaai. I was eager to hear this story, to add to my own times with the Masaai. It turned out to be a presentation by an articulate twenty-five year old who told of the customs of his tribe.

"My name is George. I am Masaai. I am from this region. Masaai believe we came from the sky. With the cow. Cow is important because is livelihood. We depend on cow for everything." He said this all in his opening paragraph.

"No vegetables," he said standing, leaning on one leg. "No fruits," he continued, his exemplary trim, fit body supported by his tall stick. "Fruits are for baboons." The intimate, small group laughed. "Don't eat veggies or cereals," he looked directly at the small audience of Germans, Americans and others. "Eat only products from cow," he paused and considered his feet before continuing.

"Meat, milk, blood," he looked in my direction. "Sometimes mix." Now he crossed one leg in front of the other. "This makes Masaai tall and strong." He stood even more erect. "Most are tall. If short, drink blood and mix," as he spoke he smoothed the front of his red Masaai blanket-sarong.

"No mattress," he started a new paragraph. "Sleep on cow skin; on hide."

Sex in the Savannah

In the morning, camp breakfast included a buffet, make that a table, of cold choices: doughy crepes, cold Spanish omelets, cold baked beans and cold bacon, the fat congealed on the tray, everything dished up hours before. "You guys have waffles?" from the Mormon boy.

We spent the day on game drives with Bernard.

"No animals today." This was not what we wanted to hear from our driver. It was his job to locate the game, to find out from other drivers where the illusive wildlife migrated overnight.

Animals remained sparse, elusive. Finally, we spotted one lone ostrich, maybe guarding the eggs. Nearby, small plovers and sand pipers tiptoed on pink-orange toothpick legs like walking hors d' oeuvres alongside Big Bird.

Later we saw several elephant herds though few bulls. We also saw grey-brown oryx, their victory horns rising to the sky, and gazelle. A small pride of four lions lounged, about six kilometers from the vehicle.

"Ah, look. Lion." Bernard leaned out his window. He bragged about this as if he were a premier driver of some kind. Maybe, if we stayed twenty-four to forty-eight hours they might amble toward the van. We used the binoculars to see the brown fluffs on the horizon.

We saw nothing extraordinary, but enjoyed the therapeutic viewing.

By the end of the day, we noted five different prides of lion including the honeymooners. Okay, nature is nature, but I'm not all that enamoured by watching sex in the savannah for hours. Bernard seemed mesmerized and turned off the engine to witness the dashing around in the high grass: the not-tonight sequence, the conqueror episode, the penetration; he, Bernard, leaning forward over his steering wheel, always, to get a better view.

Finally, we drove off and spotted male and female kudu though not together. Daryle maintained a fondness for greyish greater kudu and loved guesstimating the length, or is it height, of the rack. How does one measure the swirl of the horn, especially from the pop top of the van? Regardless, even the novice traveler appreciated the beauty in the simple double twist of the spikes emanating from the centre of the skull.

"Measuring for record-setting is a triangulated effort." Daryle sounded professorial. "You measure from the skull to the tip of the horn," he said gesturing out the window, "and again from the widest bend in the curvature." He once shot a kudu; it seemed like a good idea at the time; the time was different. Since then, fifty years ago, our attitudes have changed; the times have changed.

Today, safari is about shooting wildlife with a camera, not a gun. Safari is about viewing: stopping the car, offing the engine, adjusting the glasses. Safari is about observation; the expedition is about understanding animal behaviours, social behaviours. Perhaps a photo is possible, perhaps there is time to rough sketch before the animal wanders off, or rough draft on a yellow pad or tablet.

Safari is like hovering, waiting, observing during a scuba dive; watching the school dart one direction then, in synchronized movement, left turn away in perfect unison, darting together.

★ ★ ★

After dinner, we talked more with Masaai Man. I asked him again about the religion.

"All Masaai and cows come down from the sky," he repeated,

not deviating from his original explanation. "Masaai are only in Kenya and Tanzania," he said looking into the fire, then back at me. "We are free to wander without passport between the two countries," he stated almost robotically. "Masaai must always do good. There is no written code but they," he used third person plural, "they learn through oral tradition." He continued, "They may take cattle of any other tribe because all cattle belong to Masaai." I tried to follow this thinking.

"There are codes that they know." He continued to use the third person plural. This was new information for me, in terms of codes. "You cannot sleep with a wife of your father's age group." Seemed obvious, but it was a code. "No problem if you sleep with someone's wife from your own age group." Age groups are formed at youth and continue through their circumcision, manhood, and through elder-hood. My interpretation: they could sleep around; no allegiance.

"The punishment for this offense," sleeping with someone's wife from your father's age group, "is *curse*." This is not a crime, the Masaai said. "Stealing and murder are crimes," he said, emphasizing clarification between the two, "and the case goes before a tribunal if there is enough evidence." I wondered, is guilt the root, the cause of curse?

Masaai man continued in a poetic style.

"Masaai in only Kenya and Tanzania. No passports. We are nomadic pastoralists.

"We keep the animals.

"We wander.

"Wander because of cow.

"We look for grass and water.

"Land in Masaai is owned by community. Not one person.

"Forty-two tribes in Kenya." He lacked verbs. "For Masaai you only take cows in Masaai land," he affirmed, "not from Uganda or Somalia or any other country. Have exams. From childhood and adulthood." He went on to explain. "One examination: if boy, after circumcision, you are a man. For girl, a woman; circumcision not done in hospital but in village." He must have explained this often; it was not a western concept. "Many boys together. Twenty to fifty boys." He referred to the age group. "Traditional doctor, not from hospital. Nothing ease the pain. Can't show fear because you are known as fearful and no girl will marry."

Someone asked, "Why for girls, the circumcision?" This went unanswered.

"Then boys go to the savannah for three years. Stay and don't come back; and learn. Medicine with herbs. Traditional medicine men. How to kill lion. Not with gun but with spear. Learn discipline, how to respect the elders." This seemed like a useful concept. Send all the little boys off until they become reasonable adults. Something like *Lord of the Flies* with a positive outcome.

The conversation shifted to marriage and how to care for wives.

"The warriors, Moran, come back to the village after three years on the savannah," Masaai Man continued. "Their hair is long," he looked wistfully into the fire as if pining for those days as an independent guy with his mates. "They do not shave their long hair and are called Moran, warriors. After this period of time alone they are no longer warriors and their mothers shave their long hair." As the group end their three years he explained that all the warriors come together as an age group and shave the long hair.

Now they are given license to become married. According to Masaai man, it seems they don't like this process and some cry because it signals the end of fun and start of responsibility: marriage and responsibility.

Masaai Man talks to us about marriage. "First wife is arranged." He looks around at the non-African group. "The father will look for beautiful girl. Will speak with parents of girl then, girl must be circumcised." He says this as if it is the most natural thing in the world. "Then girl is brought to village of the Masaai young boy. They start a family. Dowry normally 10 cows from the boy's family to the girl's family. No cows: no wife. Then for second wife polygamy. One man can have many wives. No *matata*." He looks at all of us, "Must be rich."

"*My* choice for second wife," he emphasized that he makes the choice this time, "choose a Masaai friend and together go looking and visit villages searching for beautiful girl then don't talk with girl, but talk with parents." He discussed this as if trolling the malls for a pair of Nikes.

"If okay, then give ten cows, then girl must be circumcised," he repeats. "Then we, with my friends collect the girl. Girl is circumcised and she goes to village to be second wife. Friend goes back to his village. They're not dealers." I swear he read my mind.

"Wives make own house. Wife one, wife two, when friend comes he comes with his spear then puts at entrance of second wife then sleeps there. I don't go. He is my friend and deserves this. If pregnant, baby becomes husbands, not friend's baby. Best friend, best man, should be married and must not come every day." The men in the western audience nod and consider the possibilities of this custom.

"One cow one-hundred dollars. Can take another woman from another tribe and woman becomes Masaai." He answered a question from the guests.

Again someone asked, "Why circumcision of ladies?"

"Good reason. Polygamy many wives. This is done to bring down temperature of woman." I stifle a gasp. "Husband has six wives," he explains as if this is the most natural thing in the world, "bring feelings down of house."

"Responsibility of men and women," he summarizes. "Women milk cows, get water from river, bring fire wood to village, cook, bear children. Men's work: take care of family. Well-fed with meat. Cows belong to father. He makes babies, makes a mama full. Papa sleeps during the day. At night papa is busy with wives." The men laugh at this with a hardy laugh. The women laugh with sad understanding.

Is Sex for Fun or Procreation?

M asaai Man ended his discussion, appropriately, talking about their death culture. "Masaai don't bury the dead," he said as we all paused. I sensed I knew where this was going. "Remove clothing, ornaments." He looked at me sideways. "Take to savannah for hyena and jackals. Don't dig soil because soil gives grass for cows," he leaned on his stick, "then milk and meat." I was reminded of a cross-stitch pattern which quoted: Patience. Remember the cow. In time even the grass becomes milk.

"Masaai drink blood and mix in milk." He dragged his walking stick in the soft dirt as if drawing. "Don't kill cow to get blood. Take from jugular vein with arrow and get blood." A few squirmed at this notion. "Use cow dung to stop bleeding." Masaai Man was a person of few words. At least in English he seldom used a subject and a verb in the same sentence.

"Donkey only for transport not food. Only eat meat from cow, sheep," he ticked the meals off on the fingers of his left hand, "goat."

He seemed to summarize the next topics. "Ankai is god and good. If you are good, good things happen to you." Was this a version of 'God helps those who help themselves?'

"Ceremonies for everything. For circumcision, when baby is born, for marriage, every occasion is ceremony." It took me back to India with a plethora of religions promising a celebration every day.

"Was sex for fun or procreation?" The discussion around the campfire generated by the Germans and Swiss became lively. It was an amusing group of young couples. Masaai Man tossed the question back to them, what did *they* think? The men voraciously agreed, sex was for fun; well, also for procreation. Masaai Man agreed it was enjoyable but mostly, he leaned toward reproduction.

He hinted at the problem of infant mortality. Countless young mothers die at childbirth, though large families are common; this attitude of naiveté remains a major concern regarding population issues in Kenya. No one mentioned family planning or birth control in this country of a statistically high, alarming population growth rate.

In the morning we headed out with coffee and the lumbering Bernard. Thank God for the coffee. After hours and hours of random driving, round and around, north, south, east, west I spotted a lone vulture atop a scrawny tree. A small herd of oryx and zebra foraged beyond.

Three jackal cautiously, nervously, cantered along the side of the road. Aha. This could be of interest. "Bernard," I bellowed from my row of seats. "Stop the van." He turned around thinking I was about to be sick. "I want to watch these dogs," I said partly to see if he would respond to my encyclopedic knowledge of wildlife. He slowed the vehicle.

"These are not dogs, Madam," he announced. "These are very rare wild jackals." He leaned over the back seat to make his point. Bernard should have signed up for the circus; his name should have been Barnum. He must think, "There's a sucker born every minute."

As we waited, a lion approached and chased the jackal off. He drug something along; zebra kill. Of course Bernard could not explain the behaviors: a single lion, a single vulture, three jackal. This seemed unusual to me. The whole scenario seemed different. Usually, lion live together in prides and hunt in groups at night. And usually, the females carryout the hunt. The lion was maneless but a male, a single male.

The protective tomcat held off the approaching jackals, their scent detectors already on the overload; the vulture stood no chance, yet. Struggling, the single lion alone, with no help from any pride members, strained to drag the bloodied, limp mass of black and white but did not, could not, move far. He rested then lunged his teeth into the neck, then the stomach and soft innards which he sucked and licked and chewed. Exhausted, he rested again, satisfied for the moment.

Bernard told us nothing. He knew the animal names; I knew the animals: zebra, giraffe, buffalo, kudu. It's not difficult. But I know little of their habitats, behavior or patterns and I don't know the birds. Too bad for this lost opportunity. I'm beginning to think that after years of safari, years of bush trips, I could almost do as well as Bernard. I need to brush up on Swahili.

After the sighting he drove fifteen minutes to get another view; too far. He drove back to the original spot. We observed a few minutes then *halas*, finished, enough. Off we went. When Daryle protested, Bernard said, "Oh no, Bwana. Must return to camp soon, far from the gate."

How could we learn the process of animal behaviors if we couldn't observe? We wanted to watch the jackal sneak up and get their share of the meal, wanted to see how the vultures approached. Grrr. We drove three hours tracking the lion, observed fifteen minutes. Insane.

Our final night at the bush camp the staff set our table at the campfire with white linen. The food was the same. Uninspired: dry, overcooked chicken with a mound of dry, white rice. This was a budget tour, I didn't need to remind myself. The idea behind budget was that we could come more often if we traveled bottom-of-the-line.

The men of the camp joined us for post dinner conversation as we moved from our table to camp chairs around the fire. This time the discussion was not centered on the Masaai. It started with a dialogue about the deserted Aruba Lodge. We have known the lodge over the years, but this year found it nearly abandon with a skeleton staff of Indian management. Daryle has always liked the facility and became inspired about opening the Lodge to bring in conservation groups. We discussed students, marketing, sales, education camps, summer camps, spring breaks for teenagers and winter breaks with so much potential for the international schools and for day trips with local schools.

As the fire crackled, I asked about what seemed to me to be the unusual kill which we drove upon in the morning. Bernard provided no answers, no explanation, did not acknowledge that it might be infrequent. Masaai Man confirmed that yes, the female lions do make the kills, but it was not unusual for a male to be excommunicated from his family. The pride, constantly challenged at mating season in particular, ferreted out the weakest males forcing them to leave the group. Prides of bachelors also have challenges and the frailest are mandated to exist alone; they must hunt solo. Yes, Masaai Man reconfirmed, a single male could bring down a young zebra unaided because the whole herd was there, the young so vulnerable.

Bernard tried to dominate the conversation and was exposed by his lack of knowledge. The topic moved to culling and legalized hunting. Masaai Man recently read an article which discussed this possibility for Kenya and he agreed that it had merit. Bernard said it would never work because if you gave one person a license to kill one animal, twenty or thirty or fifty would come in and kill fifty each. It wouldn't work. The other men disagreed but Bernard was adamant. They were quiet. Bernard left and the discussion took a more relevant turn.

We discussed politics in 2004: George Bush, Tony Blair and Mwai Kibaki in Kenya and the inherent corruption in all governments. "This government is corrupt," someone said of Kenya.

"They're all corrupt," I said. Daryle cringed at this, his scotoma to a perfect USA exposed. All of the men were well read and current with international issues. Stimulated by informed conversation, we finally crashed just before the generator went out at eleven.

The Mormon family, the personification of the 'Ugly Americans' moved on and I wondered if the matron of the family converted her guide and all the others she met in Kenya. I wondered if she learned the answers to her research questions, "Yes, I'm doing research to compare Muslim and Christian attitudes toward the AIDS virus." The Germans and Swiss debating pleasure versus procreation headed out along the bumpy roads.

The next morning we also moved out. It was a long drive back to Nairobi, six and a half hours of horrible driving. Bernard claimed yesterday he saw a black mamba. Right. By this time, any hope of a congenial relationship deteriorated. He dropped us off at the Hotel Six-Eighty, pocketed his tip and left; a wasted opportunity.

All was not lost. At the Norfolk Hotel we reveled in a late and final luxury gourmet lunch of fresh greens and white fish enhanced with dry white wine. The Norfolk smacks of colonial luxury: old, elegant, tasteful. We lavished in it; we deserved it before for a four-thirty morning wakeup call for our confirmed, eleven-movie flight for reentry to America. Again.

Moses and
the Chief of Police

Military vehicles surrounded the large presidential villa after sealing off Entebbe International Airport. The army seized control of Radio Uganda and Idi Amin spoke to the nation announcing his takeover. Villagers across the nation took to the streets in jubilation and celebration. Milton Abote was out as president of Uganda and Idi Amin became the third ruler, soon to be despot, of the country, January 1971.

* * *

Moses Mbelle's western wardrobe put some teachers to shame. Impeccably dressed he wore beautiful cotton shirts with button-down collars, not tee shirts but dress shirts and sport shirts always tucked in. He sported dark slacks and spit-polished dress shoes all week shifting to upscale designer jeans on the weekend.

Moses was a driver and knower-of-all-things in Kampala. He is a big part of the history of the International School of Uganda and because of his keen mind, shared the wisdom of his insight when asked. It was on a trip to Ziwa Rhino Sanctuary on the outskirts of Kampala that I learned of his background and life during the rule of the infamous Idi Amin.

Moses and his eleven siblings lived in the same house in the village not far from their uncle. His father, a respected public servant worked as a police officer. Through diligence, honesty and long hours he became head of the police department. Moses, his brothers, sisters and parents were a large and close family.

When Idi Amin staged a military coup d'état in 1971 people in Kampala and major cities of Uganda celebrated the change of government. Amin, while lacking a formal education, possessed an intuitive sense of leadership. He spoke gently, then came down with a counterpoint heavy-handedness. Amin said in his first speech following his takeover, "I am not a politician but a professional soldier. I am, therefore, a man of few words and I have been brief through my professional career."

The new president went about killing anyone suspected of being part of the opposition. He and his collaborators systematically as well as randomly murdered his opponents one by one.

It was after one of his killings, after shooting down an opponent, that Amin's men went to the police and ordered them to falsify the records so that it would look like an accident, a car accident.

"I can't do that," Police Chief Mbelle said flatly. "The man was shot in the chest."

"You must produce the official police certificate." The henchman continued, "You must write on police stationery that this man died in a car accident."

"Are you are asking me to compromise my position as Chief of Police? My entire department will be compromised." Not willing to back down he continued, "The death certificate must come from the government hospital."

"You must do as the President suggests." He took a step closer, puffing out his chest. "You must declare that this man died in a car accident. You have the authority to do this," he persisted.

"Sir, with respect, I have the authority of the people of this district to uphold the laws and protect the citizens." Police chief, Mbelle stood his ground. "You cannot ask me go against the moralities of our good people, of our good country."

"Do you have a family?"

"Of course and I hold to my principles for my family as well as this village whom I serve."

"Do you expect to see your family again?"

Mbelle showed no outward emotion though his heart pounded until he thought the badge on his chest might fall to the wooden floor.

"With respect Sir," he repeated, "it would not be circumspect for the papers to be altered. I'm sure the President, Sir, would agree."

"If you do not comply, you will not see your family." He did not raise his voice. "You have many sons, isn't it?" He continued, "A pity not to see them grow up and serve our good nation."

Police Chief Mbelle was abducted from his office. Moses was seven.

* * *

That day as he bounded home from school Moses noticed a group of men gathered at his house along the path and inside his home. They hovered around the front in the gravel, men who were unfamiliar, unknown. He saw them from the lane as he jogged, his athletic legs bounding across puddles as he neared the house. He didn't recognize any of them; he quickly diverted and went to his uncle's home nearby.

The family, his brothers and his mother were violently threatened. The unknown men ransacked the house. They went through closets, drawers and desks tossing papers and files across the floor. The disruption overwhelmed the family. Chief of Police Mbelle did not return. Devastated and terrified, the family moved in with their mum's brother. Uncle Joseph, who rearranged his home to accommodate his sister's large family, offered stability.

As they abandon their home they snatched what was left of their clothes strewn across the floor. They gathered valuable papers and personal identity cards as they found them crumpled and disbursed across the cement floors and stuffed them into black rubbish bags to be sorted at a later time. Everything of value was looted including watches, the radio, typewriter, jewelry and silverware.

They waited for word from Police Chief Mbelle. Mrs. Mbelle went to the police station daily begging for information. None was forthcoming. The officers could only report to her what they witnessed. Every day Uncle Joseph jumped on the back of a *boda boda* motor bike dodging potholes, traveling highways and back roads to search and inquire at the prisons in the region. If anyone possessed information, they were reluctant or unable to tell him anything.

After three months of continued harassment, and no word of the police chief, Moses, his mother and several siblings packed boiled eggs and mashed green banana *matoke* and took passage by bus to escape to Kenya.

"Where are we going?"

"When will we come back?"

"Why do we need our bed rolls? Are we sleeping in Kenya?"

"Will Papa be there? Will we meet him in Kenya?"

"Can't we stay with Uncle Joseph?"

"When can we go back to our house? I don't want to go to another house."

"Are we there yet, Mama?"

"Why do we have to go? What about our friends? Where are we going?"

"When can we come back?"

Along the way they purchased boiled peanuts from the window of the bus and oranges. At one village stop they bought hot fresh grilled corn on the cob from vendors fanning their charcoal at the side of the road. Inside the bus chickens cackled, one man cradled a goat and a small woman wrestled a pig whose feet had been cobbled. They bounced along the rutted road to an uncertain future.

"We're going to see Robert." His oldest brother already lived and worked in Kenya as a teacher. In order to maximize their limited resources they stayed outside the city in a small village near the border.

According to Moses, who remembers the details from a child's perspective, they immediately traveled to Nairobi to begin the process of obtaining refugee status. Back on a bus again, they bounced their way into the bustling chaos of Nairobi. Mrs. Mbelle, dragging her gaggle of children, made her way in and out of offices set up to assist the influx of Ugandans. Sitting at wooden tables she meticulously filled out forms, while the children sat on the floor drawing on the back of recycled papers. She methodically went through the logistics of establishing refugee status.

They stayed in one room in an inexpensive hotel for several weeks during the process. She applied for aide and through the

Kenyan government did receive financial assistance.

"Yes, I will come with you. You will meet new friends." Mrs. Mbelle enrolled Moses and his brothers in the local Kenyan primary school. But when he came home in the late afternoon, Moses cried.

"They don't speak the same words," he sobbed. "I don't know what the teacher is saying," he lifted his hands to hide his face. "When she writes on the board, I can't read the words. I don't understand," he cried in frustration.

The teacher spoke and taught in Kiswahili, not English or Luganda. Moses and his brother shared a desk and tried to fumble their way through the day. He was lost, not knowing what the teacher was trying to explain. The teacher was equally frustrated. He was young and confused. They did not make friends the first day. He felt alone, displaced. He kicked a plastic ball around the street, best friends with his brothers. Robert worked in the secondary school and tried to console his siblings.

Moses and his brother enjoyed the maths, until they were asked to read the word problems. Slowly, the boys unlocked the sounds and symbols word by word and were eventually conversant in Kiswahili.

They longed for letters from Uncle Joseph. When the mail arrived, Mrs. Mbelle carried the unopened letter to her hotplate. She boiled a pot of water and made a strong cup of African tea. After pouring in a dollop of milk she sat in the one soft chair. She turned the envelope over several times appreciating the familiar handwriting of her brother.

She took a sip of tea and slowly slit the envelope with the edge of the kitchen knife. "My Dear Sister," he always began. He told of atrocities occurring in Uganda. He told her that Idi Amin expelled the Asian population of Indians and Pakistanis. He told her that the Asian shops closed and did not reopen; that the companies and factories and agricultural farms they owned and managed no longer functioned, that the economy was on the edge collapse. He told her Amin could not feed his soldiers, that they were given permission to poach, kill and eat the wildlife in national reserves; that the kob population was already nearly extinct. He told her that abductions and murders continued. There was never a word about the whereabouts of the Chief of Police. It seemed he vanished. Mrs. Mbelle suspected the truth but never allowed herself the anguish of formulating the horrible conclusion.

They stayed in Kenya for two years until the civil unrest quelled. When Moses returned to Uganda with his family, everything was gone, lost to the government, the property confiscated. Their house was taken over, their personal belongings looted. Once again they started over, once again with Uncle Joseph.

The boys rejoined their former classmates and friends but there was little income for the family to survive. High education fees, the cost of uniforms and contributing to the family food pantry led to more cups of tea and more family discussion. They moved back to the village along the shores of Lake Victoria.

His mother started a fish business and became a fish monger selling at the wet market in the large fishing village. As a former local resident she knew the villagers who welcomed them home. Early each morning she met the boats as they came ashore and brought the fresh fish from Lake Victoria to sell at her small stall. Every day she scanned the shoppers for a glimpse, a hope of her beloved, lost husband.

The boys registered for classes in the local school and when Moses completed secondary school with honours he made his way back to Kampala and worked his way up a chain of positions. When I met him he was well appointed in beautiful shirts and slacks and looking very smart.

Today, his mother travels to Kampala for short visits with her sons and grandchildren. The story of Moses is the only one I heard, told to me in first person. During the eight years of Idi Amin's rule it is estimated that three to five-hundred-thousand Ugandans disappeared or were murdered and were never seen or heard from again.

Obama and Nandi

"I'm not getting anything done." The Mister pushed back from his computer and shut it down; the battery was low. Mizz Dannie and her Mister lived in the suburbs of Kampala, only a short drive to the bush, the outback, game territory. "I need to write reports and there is no power. I can't get this done. There's no water. No showers. No power. No internet. No local news or international. No refrigerator. No food."

"We love Africa, remember?" Mizz Dannie understood his frustration.

"I can't get anything *done*," he repeated. As usual, the Mister brought work home on the weekend. As usual he was frustrated by the lack of amenities at the house. There was a noisy generator, but there was seldom any gaz available to run it.

"You know what?" Mizz Dannie slipped into valley-talk, "Let's blow this joint." Then added, "We've never been to the Rhino Sanctuary. Let's flee da scene; let's go check it out."

* * *

Driving on the outskirts of Kampala, they passed small kiosks, the names worthy of note:

Feel Free Pub,
Gadhafi Battery Service,
Mogas Petrol Station,
All Faith's *Islamic* School.

The busses carried messages on the front windshield or the back bumper, sometimes on the sides of the bus. Mizz Dannie read them out as they passed.

"God is Great," she recited. "God Never Fails." She bounced with the potholes. "God Is Able."

"I can read, thank you, Mizz Dannie," the Mister kept his eyes on the road.

"I can't help it, I have to read them out. It's a full Sunday sermon written on the buses,"

she said gawking out the window. "Did you see that one 'Oh Jesus.'?" A double-decker bus coming directly toward them carried the label, People's Arc. "I bet the driver is called Noah." She decided "Groly Be To God" was the best.

They proceeded on with Moses driving and weaving through the traffic. She particularly liked the Tic Hotel. Was this truth in advertising? Next to it was the 'Taste Me Take Away.' Next to that a popular Uganda chain called 'I Feel Like Chicken Tonight.'

★ ★ ★

It was green. It was clean. It was quiet. Mizz Dannie and the Mister registered at the sanctuary office and looked around the grounds of the reserve.

"Look! Spring Bok wandering in and out, not spooked at all," Mizz Dannie whispered.

"If you would like a hot lunch, we can offer you roast chicken," the hostess offered, "then you can head out with a guide at two thirty." That sounded perfect.

After lunch, the Mister and Mizz Dannie met the guide, who jumped in the front seat with Moses.

"Jhambo, my name es Jaj. I be your guide."

"Jambo, Jaj." The skinny Ugandan, carried a skinny rifle; Jaj was a long, tall, wildlife ranger who worked permanently at the Rhino Sanctuary.

"It's Jaj. You ready to go? We see the rhino."

"Oh, *George*. Sorry." Mizz Dannie, grateful to be in the back seat without the rifle or the deodorant-free guide, peered between their shoulders, her binoculars swinging from her neck.

"What happened to the Rhino in Uganda?" Mizz Dannie leaned forward addressing George.

"All gone now Mizz. Only the ones he-aah, we protect."

"But what happened to them?" She knew the answer, however was curious how this conservationist might present the story.

Once, she knew, thousands of rhinos wandered across non-existent borders traversing East Africa, Central and Southern Africa. Poaching and hunting took a toll on the tally. In Uganda, in the 1960's there were still 400 Eastern Black Rhinos in Kidepo Valley and 300 Northern White Rhinos in the West Nile and Murchison Falls National Park.

During the terrible unrest with President Idi Amin, all the wildlife suffered. Elegant African cranes, fish eagles, secretary birds, spotted quail, wild turkey, even vultures and other bird-life were shot to supply meals for the army; gazelle, impala, kudu killed for military meals, elephant killed for the ivory and rhino slain for the horns. The last rhino seen in Uganda was in 1983.

"Bad man, Idi Amin. Kill all Uganda wildlife; he kill people too."

"I read that Uganda lost seventy-five percent of the elephants, nearly all of the crocodiles, eighty percent of the lions and leopards plus all of the rhinos when Amin was here."

"Mr. Amin, he no care," he pronounced it kay-ah. "Poachas make big money, maybe Mr. Amin too. Ziwa Rhino Sanctuary nice place foh rhino to live. Ha! Five stah hotel foh rhino," George enjoyed his joke.

The Rhino Fund Uganda was established in 1997 Mizz Dannie read. Four years later they raised funds to relocate two rhinos to Uganda.

"When they raised funds enough for two rhinos, why did they place them in the zoo?" She was shocked that the Rhino were not placed in the natural environment.

"Es goo question, Madam. Da zoo es nice, Madam. You see in Entebbe?"

"Yes, we have been there and the environment is very natural, I agree," she said and leaned in to the front seat. "But why," Mizz Dannie did not understand this, "when they finally got enough capital," she clarified, "enough money to fund two rhinos, why place them in the zoo?" She queried the ranger. "Why not place them in their natural surroundings?" It didn't make sense to Mizz Dannie.

George explained in broken English that the Fund was established to work in collaboration with communities and villages. The mission of the zoo, the Uganda Wildlife Education Centre in Entebbe, was to raise awareness. The centre was open for the public and encouraged school trips for children.

Their aim was to spend the necessary years academically reintroducing the rhino to villagers: to teach the importance of sustaining the population of the rhino, the importance to Uganda to bring in visitors and the virtue of reinstating the reputation of the country.

They bounced along the dirt trails, Moses and George in the front, the Mister and Mizz Dannie in the back. "Go he-ahh," George directed Moses. "Too much mud. Can get stuck they-aah." We swerved in the slick sludge.

In 2005 four white rhinos were relocated from Kenya to Ziwa Rhino Sanctuary.

"America donated two white rhinos. Hyou 'Merikhani?"

"How is that?" Mizz Dannie lifted one eyebrow. "We don't have rhinos in America. Did someone send a donation?"

"Disney Animal Kingdom, in Flo-ri-dah give two rhino."

The Disney rhinos arrived in October 2006 making a total of six rhino now in Uganda. Three males and three females settled in and all three females produced calves making a total of nine rhinos at the start of 2010.

"We call first four rhinos from Kenya, Taleo and Moja, the

males, Bella and Kori the females. The two rhinos from 'Merikha we call Hasani the male and Nandi the female. In 2010, all rhinos about 10 years old."

Naming the rhinos made it all seem like family. Each was identified by a nick on the ear, a scar or other markings. We pulled the car into a clearing beside tall trees.

"Let's go," George jumped out of the car.

"What!" Mizz Dannie sat stunned. She looked at her Mister.

"We go very quiet. We no talk now," George wore forest green walking shorts which exposed his long, tall frame.

"We're walking? Out of the car? With the rhino? Walk-ing? No way."

George held the door for Mizz Dannie. Most game parks implore: Do not get out of your vehicle at any time. Violators will be fined.

"First calf born at Ziwa Sanctuary was to Nandi," George told us, walking alongside The Mister. "Baby born in Africa of 'Merikhan mother and Kenya father." Then, "We call him Obama. That was June 24, 2009." The Mister laughed too loud. "Maybe we find Obama and Nandi today."

"W-walking?" Mizz Dannie quivered as she spoke.

Out of the car, and processing the idea that they were now one with nature, Mizz Dannie picked up a walking stick from the ground. The Mister charged ahead following George closely. Moses stayed back with Mizz Dannie, resisting the urge to run.

"Now no talking." George instructed. "When we see rhino, look for near tree."

"You're kidding," Mizz Dannie said under her breath. "You mean *climb* the tree?"

"Must always be ready. Rhino wild animal." He spoke softly, adjusting the shoulder strap of his rifle. "Rhino do not see so well," he turned around to face us, "but they have very good sense of smell. You take bath today?" still in low tones. "Ha! I make joke." Mizz Dannie did not laugh.

"When we find rhino, no make move quick," George instructed. Mizz Dannie tiptoed, undecided whether to be close to the guide, and therefore closer to the impending rhino, or at the end of their Congo line and a bit farther from the intended sighting.

"You must be 'a-we-ah of otha wild animals and snakes." As if rhino wasn't enough. "No step on branches or twigs." In the *forest*?

"*This is impossible,*" she thought. "*They will smell us before they see us. Hear us before we see them. Look for a tree; make your way to its branches without moving quickly; make no swift movements. Impossible.*" Her heart pounded pa-boom, pa-boom.

After some time walking through tall grasses and stepping over broken twigs George said, "We getting close now." He mumbled softly into his walkie-talkie like a security person at the airport, then back to us, "Nando and Obama," he whispered, "in those bushes under trees. See they-ah? We come back. Maybe they move."

Pa-boom, pa-boom, Mizz Dannie's heart thundered. Why did this seem like a good idea? Had anyone ever died here? Would she and her Mister be the first? She held back; the gap between them grew as she slowed behind George. Mizz Dannie composed the headline for her obituary, *Expatriate Living In Uganda Gored and Trampled on Walking Safari. Rhino Acquitted.*

Mizz Dannie thought of the rhinos at the Entebbe Zoo, beyond a deep trench; at the time she didn't like the idea that the first two rhinos were in a zoo and not in the wild. Now, on reflection, it seemed rather better that they lived on one side of the mote and the public observed from a safe distance.

"Who are *they*?" Mizz Dannie noticed two armed men wearing forest green camouflage suits sporting hefty rifles and clip boards.

"Each rhino has round-the-clock 24/7 protection. The guards make notes and document movement and behavior," George explained in more fluent language. "It's for protection against poachers and also for research." Mizz Dannie leaned in to listen to the soft spoken homily, absorbed in the information briefly unaware that she was getting closer to the rhinos.

"When do the guards sleep?" she asked. It was a stupid question, she knew, but couldn't get enough of the new experience.

"The guards work four hour shifts and sleep in lodgings on the property." The guide was on a roll now with uninterrupted knowledge about his subject the rhinos and Ziwa Rhino Sanctuary. The guides, well trained and conversant, informed and educated, presented relevant information to curious and naive visitors.

"Behind those trees," he whispered, "you see them?" Mizz Dannie automatically slowed her steps to tip-toes. Two boulders stood in a small open meadow.

"Now no talk." They were silent except for the pounding pa boom, pa boom of Mizz Dannie's insides. An unseen bird screeched as it flew by. She wanted to stop right there. They were close enough, but the guide moved closer. Mizz Dannie held her breath as she scanned the open area for the nearest tree. *How would I get up that tree? Maybe I can just squat down and hide behind it?*

The guide moved forward. Closer and closer. *This is madness,* she thought. She clenched her fists tight till her nails embedded her wet palms. Mizz Dannie looked over her shoulder. Her Mister was there and edged anxiously forward behind her. She talked to herself, *He can run. Mister is a track man; he's probably safe.* Continuing the self-talk, *I'll just have a peek then tip-toe back.*

They circled behind the bushes to the side of the two rhinos who kept their flat square jaws against the ground as they foraged. She saw visually why they are called White Rhino, white a corruption of the South African or Afrikaans word for wide. The guide, Mizz Dannie and the Mister were a mere five meters from three tons each of Southern White Rhino.

George turned to face them, his back to the mammals. Mizz Dannie grabbed the elbow of her Mister but he broke away to focus his camera. "Don't use a flash, Mister," she whispered though it was broad daylight. "Here, let me take your picture with the rhino," he whispered back. Then, "Take mine." Then to George, "Would you take our photo?" This was a flashback to early tourists in Kenya who snapped photos then roared off to the next photo-op without observation or reflection. It seemed then, it was all about the photo, not about the experience.

George quietly told us "White rhino can run up to 45 km per hour." Quickly calculating, Mizz Dannie registered 28 mph, faster than the limit in a school zone. "Oh man," she looked at the nearest tree, a limp acacia which would never support her even if she could shinny up the trunk.

Sighting the rhino, standing, walking, grazing, sitting complacent: beautiful. This was not a YouTube video; not a Wikipedia report. Mizz Dannie wanted to be brave, wanted to learn. Self-talk got her through the walking expedition. Now, she was in the moment.

The rhino lifted its head, turned slightly to look to the side. Mizz Dannie froze, then instinctively stepped backward. "Oh my, puleeze don't hear my heart," pa boom, pa boom it rattled around in her chest.

It was like taking a step back in time, prehistoric time. She marveled at their survival, but for the possession of their coveted horns. Some countries had shaved off the horns; the marauders murdered the rhinos in defiance. As if reading her mind George said, "Four rhinos killed in South Africa last week. Three males; no more breeding stock, no sperm bank. This very sad."

He talked in muffled tones into his walkie-talkie. "We go now, again see Baby Obama and Nandi. Walk slowly and no talk as we leave."

In the silent trek to locate the American mother and her African son, Mizz Dannie reflected, grateful for the vision at Ziwa Sanctuary, appreciative of those who valued the relevance of saving the species, indebted to those who made this vision available to the common person. A roller bird flashed from a lower branch displaying lilacs, azure blues, greens and cinnamon in a glorious spin like a whirling dervish.

"There they are, Madam. Obama and Nandi. You like?" He spoke with his hand to his mouth to muffle the sound. Obama sat in the grass near Nandi who foraged with her square wide mouth and jaw. She moved slowly away from us, but George followed at a respectful distance, Mizz Dannie still lagging behind. She knew rhino could be aggressive, especially when protecting their young. She was filled with adrenalin like a tight rope walker crossing to safety, still terrified that she was doing this back-to-nature thing. They took more photos before George prodded them back toward the car, pointing out the names of the trees and shrubs.

On the drive back to Kampala, they bounced over the potholes, now thoroughly refreshed, energized and exhausted from the day.

"Think there will be any water when we get back?" The Mister, already thinking of home.

"I doubt it," she responded, leaning her head against the back seat. "Probably no power either. But I loved seeing those rhinos."

As they drove up the drive, the lights blazed throughout the house. "Yeah, Powah. Feel the Powah." Mizz Dannie was happy.

"I can finish my reports." The Mister was happy.

This was why they loved Africa.

Guinea Fowl

If I wanted to buy birds, I would not find them in a pet shop. I would find them at the outdoor market, Nakasero market in Uganda. The outdoor shopping quarter was large, covering numerous city blocks and offered vegetables, fruits, house wares and car parts; another sector housed the Chinese market. Behind the section of fruits and vegetables I found the birds.

Think of Nakasero as an outdoor mall, sort of. A mall where everyone seemed to want to be where you were. A mall where there were always puddles of mud. A mall without air-conditioning or store fronts. A mall that offered an abundance of merchandise from fruits and nuts to car parts and bolts.

Nakesero was not as inviting as other outdoor African markets such as the Mercado
   in Addis Ababa, reported to be the largest in Africa or
      the Khan el Khalili Bazaar in Cairo with darkish alleys and smallish stalls or
         the Berber suqs in Marrakesh offering rows and rows of ceramic tagine or
            the Stonetown market in Zanzibar, small and clean and known for spices
            and artwork, especially Naive African paintings.

Nakasero market was nothing like outdoor Asian markets such as the Grand Bazaar of
Istanbul with blocks of every possible type of merchandise or
the Afghani market in Islamabad with woven carpets, jewelry of lapis and amber,
fine pieces of blown glass, colourful embroidered caps for boys.
It was not like the vast and sprawling Chat-u-chak Market in Bangkok.
Nor was Nakasero anything like the outdoor suqs in Riyadh which boasted
Bedouin artifacts, old silver and nouveau gold for the nouveau riche.
Dirty, muddy, crowded: Nakasero always seemed depressing but
I continued to go. Some things were only available at Nakasero.

On this day I looked for guinea fowl. Daryle and I loved the unique birds from our first encounter in the Ethiopian bush. Now, living in Kampala, in an enormous, dysfunctional five bedroom house with a huge garden and outdoor bar-gazebo it seemed like the perfect place for our own guineas. It was the occasion of our 49th wedding anniversary.

The birds located in an open, though covered area, roofed with corrugated aluminium, waited.

I walked past the pineapple corner. Vendors sat with mounds of spiny, pointy pineapples and even larger mounds of pineapple tops violently hacked-off like one might imagine beheadings, all for the eager consumer; all heaped in a huge pile. The tops fermenting in the sun emitted a narcotic aroma.

I stepped over string beans; I stepped over string bean sellers who meticulously spread their skinny legumes across black plastic bags spread-out on the ground. I stepped over rows of lined up carrots; I walked around mounds of dry rice, pyramids of millet and piles of ground corn.

I found the birds, cooped up in mini wire cages. Beyond the chickens I tip-toed, carefully avoiding pools of sludge, stepping on narrow dirt lanes avoiding puddles when possible. I hobbled along scrawny mud lanes, trying not to slip, past the chickens, finally locating the guinea fowl.

The *mzungu* is always problematic. The whole bird market gathered around the *mzungu*. Why was I there in the chicken coop? What did I want? Most importantly: How much would I pay for whatever I wanted? I was the *mzungu*. White people always pay more.

In simple language: I want guinea fowl. I want two pairs: two males, two females.

Everything is negotiable. But hey! I'm good. I used to go to Tijuana and learned to bargain. Then I moved international where everything is negotiable. I'm pretty good. Years ago on home leave I went shopping with my mom in California in a big store, The May Company. I went to the counter and asked the woman at the cash register, "What's your best price." My mother was mortified.

"Dannie, the price is set by the manufacturer. She can't change the price," she said indicating the woman at the register.

"You mean the price is fixed."

"Yes. It's fixed."

"Okay, but," I said to the employee, "What is your best price? I'm sure you can make

a better price." I wanted to negotiate for guinea males, guinea females, guinea pairs; nothing is simple. But hey! I'm good. "How much for your guinea fowl?" I asked the vendor. He mumbled a price. "Why you charge so much?"

"Very special chicken," he said looking at the birds squished in the cages.

"How much for a regular chicken?" I asked. He started out with a price equivalent to about fifty dollars.

"You want chicken?"

"No. I want guinea fowl." His price was outrageous, but we had to play this game. A crowd gathered as we spoke in the narrow aisle between the chickens and guineas, the *mzungu* and the farmer.

"How many bads you want?"

"I want two male and two female," I answered. "Are these males or females?" Here I needed to rely on the vender. I had no idea by looking at these birds, but I couldn't appear to be naive. It really was a game.

"You want two bads?"

"I want four birds," I repeated the equation. "Two female and two male."

Okay, I'm good, but I don't know a male from a female guinea fowl. They all looked alike. Wattle, comb, clucking sound, size; in the end, I deferred to the owner-sellers. They, of course wanted to sell the birds. They told me anything I wanted to hear. Did I really have two pairs? Did I have two males and two females? Were the wattles different? The combs different? You know what? They all looked the same to me.

The vendor consulted with his colleague. They knew they would get a good price. I consulted with Moses, my driver, who knew less about guinea fowl than I.

"Okay, Ma'am, fifty dollah each bad."

"That's what you said before. I want four birds. You give me better price."

They put their heads together again, then, "You like this one?" he pointed to one bird.

"Yes, that's a nice bird." He separated one bird to another cage. "Is it a male or female?" We selected out three more birds, while I continued to ask, "How much for four birds?"

"I tol you, fifty dollah," and he looked back at the birds. "Okay, forty-five dollah each."

"That is too much," I reasserted. "I'm a teacher. I have little money," which was a lie because although I was a teacher I possessed significantly more money than the vendor-farmer. It was a little lie. I invented the truth. "Maybe I only buy one."

"Okay, how much you pay?"

Now it was my turn. If I quoted too low, I would insult and leave no room to negotiate. I counted on my fingers in a dramatic way. "I pay you twenty dollars per bird," I said. "That gives you eighty dollars."

He was not buying it. This was hard work. "Madam, it is not possible," he wiped his palms on his trousers. "I will lose money. I must make a little profit." He looked away again as if he was done with the negotiating.

I knew he was making a huge profit. I started to walk away, back to the car. As I walked down the path he called back, "Okay, Ma'am, eighty dollah," he said and came back to me.

The farmer and colleague grabbed each bird and bound its

ankles. We gently stuffed the birds into huge body bags and placed them in the back of the car. They jumped around in their bags, squawking all the way home.

Then I made a cage for them, an online project. I pulled from my rabbit learning experience as a kid. My father went through a period where he checked-out of the fast lane for a couple of years and went into faux farming. He built a small rabbitry on our half acre of land. He constructed rows and rows of rabbit hutches. He dug rows of ditches to handle the waste and pellets. He made aluminium feeding trays and installed individual charts in front of each cage to record reproduction efforts. He installed feed trays and hutch boxes for the does. I took it all in, not knowing that I would draw on the information at a much later time.

Now, with pencil in hand, I sketched out a small cage for the guinea fowl. It was pretty cool, actually; a pen I could assemble in the garden under the huge mango tree. I sent the driver to the highway where men-on-the-street constructed. Two hours later, the driver came back with the cage pretty much to my specs. The idea of the pen was to corral the birds in the evening.

Guinea fowl are free-range; is that what you call it wandering around our garden grounds? But how do you keep them down on the farm? How do you keep them on your property without flying off into the wild? The men on our staff decided to tie strings around some of the wing feathers. This would keep them from flying too far. That was the intention.

Anniversary gift bequeathed. The guinea fowl roamed the grounds of our property much to our delight and enjoyment. Each night when Daryle came home in the evening, we enjoyed sundowners on the upstairs deck overlooking Lake Victoria with drinks and hors d' oeuvres and 'treats' for the guinea fowl. From the balcony we tossed cracker bits or bread chunks as the fowl came running for their sundowners before being corralled into their pen.

Each evening we shooed the fowl into the cage for the night. This was mostly to protect them from vultures, even cats which roamed around in the evening looking for prey. The birds were clever about avoiding the cage; they didn't want to roost there.

It became a game coaxing the trotting, fluttering fowl into their room-with-a-view under the broad branch mango tree.

One day we found an egg in the middle of the garden, just lying in the open green grass. Well, this was exciting. Someone was laying eggs! Whoo hoo! In the middle of the garden was not cool. The next day we found another egg at the other end of the property. What's a mother to do? I decided to make a grass nest in the pen. I then placed a brown soapstone egg in the grassy nest. The next day, *voila l'affaire* a real egg. The young hen figured out she should lay her eggs in the grassy nest.

We ate the eggs for a while, very fresh and delicious for Sunday morning brunch under the thatched gazebo in the garden with the guinea fowl hovering around the table, and their cooked eggs.

We decided to see if they might hatch. According to Google, it takes 28 days for guinea fowl eggs to hatch. The female was very protective of her grassy spot, once she figured out there was a place to nest and rest. She seldom left the hovel.

The chicks started to peck and peep through the shells. The wee chicks wobbled about the grassy nest for several days then hobbled around the small pen their skinny legs plopping through the wire flooring. The mother soon led them out of the cage, a very dangerous undertaking.

She protected them well. Guinea fowl are not known to be good mums, but this one was very protective.

However, birds of prey are also good mums and one by one,
they plucked, quick as lightening,
like kids snitching cookies from the jar,
they snatched the furry little chicks
off the ground and high into the sky,
the hawks and kites jetting off
in arrogance and success.

In the end, three survived of nine hatchlings.
When we left the country, we bequeathed our beautiful,

uniquely feathered fowl to a neighbour with a flock of guineas and a huge piece of property. Of course I meticulously gathered up feathers each day: oval shaped black, and spotted with round white dots. I have several Ziplocs of the beautiful mementoes. Earrings? Perhaps, if Sir doesn't pinch them for fishing lures.

Epilogue

As outsiders, Daryle and I don't do politics. Our love of Africa includes the beaches along the Kenya coast, the Okavango Delta in Botswana and the plains and savannah of East Africa.

Chunks of Africa writhe. The world agonizes in response to mass murders in Kenya, kidnappings in Nigeria, presidential greed in Zimbabwe. Generic Africa; generic grief. Countries become causes. Causes become issues. African leadership though colourful, forces the observer, the outsider, the non-African, to pause.

While it's true some leaders come and go, others stay forever. Worldwide perception of corruption and bribery remains, as we in the West maintain our own form of fraud; we call it politics; we call it congress. We call it government.

The fortune of Goodluck is over. The influences of Museveni and Mugabe linger, each man in power nearly three decades. And still Uganda, with consistent leadership, perhaps lack of leadership, holds the title of Pothole Capital of the World. I didn't say that, they did. What is being done?

Before these monarchs, Hailie Selassie reigned in Ethiopia over four decades; poverty still reigns. Mzee Jomo Kenyatta, the academic, Pan-Africanist, founder of Kenya, ruled as Prime Minister in 1963 and President from 1964 until his death in 1978. His son, Uhuru Kenyatta, is president of Kenya today. We are more calculated. US presidential stints are limited to four years per term though we also move along family lines of political inheritance.

By contrast, Paul Kagame, President of Rwanda since 2000, is credited with ending the civil war and genocide in 1994. As a visionary he recently addressed college graduates,

> *"We must keep asking ourselves how we are using education to transform lives and in how much time. An education that does not transform your life or the life of others is a wasted education."*

—April, 2015, speaking at the University of Rwanda.

Today, African countries become causes. It's a perception. Nigeria becomes Boko Haram, *boko*: fake, fraud, inauthentic; *haram* forbidden. Loosely translated *western*, especially education, *forbidden*. Somalia becomes Al-Shabab, 'the youth.' Morocco, Maghreb, becomes Al-Qaeda, 'the base.'

Coup cartwheel; coup cartwheel; coup cartwheel coup d'état. Instability, corruption, rigged elections are newsworthy. It doesn't have to be this way; it might not be this way. Yet, perception is reality.

We love the generic Africa. We loved working in Uganda and Ethiopia. The continent gets in your blood or it does not. We became hooked on that first safari and could never get enough, even through discovery channel.

These chapters represent the oooh, ahhh elements of living, working and traveling on the continent. We loved every minute of every day, month, year; but not the power outages, the lack of water for showers; eventually, the unreliable internet access.

These episodes express reflections of our time over many years. The more frivolous experiences, though authentic, are represented by the inevitable, somewhat predictable, voice of Mizz Dannie who wishes the reader *Jambo* and *Kwaheri*.

And as the elegant elephants wander off to the waterhole, Mizz Dannie knows it's five o'clock somewhere in Africa.

CPSIA information can be obtained
at www.ICGtesting.com
Printed in the USA
FSOW01n1116130716
22694FS